Our
CEREMONY
of *Love*

The Meaning & Practice of Christian Worship

H. STEPHEN SHOEMAKER

Also by *H. Stephen Shoemaker*

Re-Telling the Biblical Story:
The Theology and Practice of Narrative Preaching
(Nashville: Broadman Press, 1985)

The Jekyll and Hyde Syndrome:
A New Encounter with the Seven Deadly Sins and Seven Lively Virtues
(Nashville: Broadman Press, 1987)

Strength In Weakness:
A Lyrical Re-Presentation of II Corinthians
(Nashville: Broadman Press, 1989)

GodStories:
New Narratives from Sacred Texts
(Valley Forge, PA : Judson Press, 1998)

Finding Jesus in His Prayers
(Nashville: Abingdon Press, 2004)

Being Christian in An Almost Chosen Nation:
Thinking About Faith and Politics
(Nashville: Abingdon Press, 2006)

Jesus Stories:
Traveling Toward Testimony
(Valley Forge, PA : Judson Press, 2016)

Seekers Saints and Sinners:
Life-Changing Encounters with Jesus
(Valley Forge, PA: Judson Press, 2019)

Baptism:
A Living Sacrament of the Christian Life
(Macon, GA: Smyth and Helwys, 2022)

Contents

Advance Praise for *Our Ceremony of Love*

If I could only give one book to a worship leader, I would present them with *A Ceremony of Love*. This is the work of a theologian-pastor-musician who understands the relentless rhythms of weekly worship. Most books on worship are written by academics who write about theory or clergy/musicians who write about practice. Stephen Shoemaker bridges these perspectives, weaving a tapestry of theology and practice of worship, diving into the why and the how of worship.

—Doug Haney
Executive Director
Polyphony Music Resources

It is startling that we Christians so seldom pay attention to the treasures in our own worship. Here Steve Shoemaker revitalizes our attention for a new day. His writing is a conversation between saints living and dead for the sake of those yet unborn. It is ecumenical in the best sense—picking up treasures wherever God has left them for us. Books don't frequently make me want to worship, but this one did.

—Jason Byassee
Senior Minister
Timothy Eaton Memorial Church in Toronto, Ontario

Smyth & Helwys Books
6316 Peake Road
Macon, Georgia 31210-3960
1-800-747-3016

Library of Congress Cataloging-in-Publication Data

Names: Shoemaker, H. Stephen, 1948- author
Title: Our ceremony of love : the meaning & practice of Christian worship /
by H. Stephen Shoemaker.
Description: Macon, GA : Smyth & Helwys Publishing, [2025] | Includes
bibliographical references.
Identifiers: LCCN 2025033776 | ISBN 9781641735940 paperback
Subjects: LCSH: Worship--History
Classification: LCC BV5 .S56 2025
LC record available at https://lccn.loc.gov/2025033776

Acknowledgements

The lovely tradition of an acknowledgments page gives me an opportunity to offer gratitude and acknowledge debt.

I first thank my wife Sue, my companion on almost every page of this book and conjuror of my better self. Without her, this book would have been much poorer, and with her, it is much better.

I am grateful to Smyth & Helwys Publishing, who agreed to support me in the journey of this book.

As to my debts, I have gratitude for people who throughout Christian history have created the liturgies of all worship traditions. I am grateful as well for those who have aided our worship of God: the writers of prayers, songs, and music. I am grateful to the reformers and renewers of worship who have done their holy work at great personal cost. I am grateful to the scholars of liturgy and theology who have taught us to pray and worship more truly. My gratitude flows toward the weekly practitioners of worship preparation and leadership who have, out of love of God, led the people of God in worship in congregations large and small in the real conditions of each congregation's life. The devoted work of these people has inspired and led me in my writing.

This book is dedicated first to my father, who initiated me into the wonder and beauty of worship. In my imagination, I can still hear him singing and see him leading a choir. Second, I dedicate this book to my colleagues in the planning and practice of worship through my ministry. No page of this book could have been written apart from them.

Finally, I thank you, God, author and audience of all our worship.

Author's Note

It was my desire to write this book using language that is as inclusive as I have the wits to use. In our day, we often stutter and stumble as we do our best to use respectful and emancipatory language. I deal with this issue most directly in chapter 17.

For this reason, I use the New Revised Standard Version as the principal translation throughout the book. Copyright © 1991, National Council of Churches of Christ in the United States of America. Used by permission. All rights reserved worldwide.

When I refer to other translations or adaptions of Scripture, I note the sources.

Our Ceremony of Love

In his short story "A Father's Story," Andre Dubus tells of a stable owner named Luke Ripley whose routine was to arise every morning before dawn for an hour of contemplation and silence with God. He carried on his conversation with God as he boiled water for coffee. There in the kitchen, he watched the light of the new day waking the world and offered it to God as a prayer of thanksgiving, prayed for those he loved past and present, and said the Lord's Prayer as "an act of faith."

Then he went to the stable with an apple or carrot for his horse. Saddling his horse, he rode him down to St. John's, the small local parish, where he took Mass with Father Paul and a few regulars. This daily routine, Dubus said, taught him "the necessity and wonder of ritual." "Ritual," he wrote, ". . . allows those who cannot will themselves out of the secular to perform the spiritual, as dancing allows the tongue-tied man a ceremony of love."[1]

This is the wonder and necessity of Christian worship. It allows us tongue-tied folks—with our fickle minds and fugitive hearts—a ceremony of love. It is more of a dance than we realize: song, the poetry of liturgy, prayer utterable and unutterable, earnest conversation with God and God's word, the offering of ourselves, and then the table of grace and benediction. In this ceremony, we join with one another and with the Christ who was and is forever the "surprise of Mercy, outgoing Gladness, Rescue, Healing and Life."[2]

In this book, I will discuss what for me is most essential and life-giving in Christian worship. In some ways, this book is a return to our origins, and in other ways, it embraces the new kind of worship the Living God evokes in us today.

In the writing of this book, I seek to transcend the "worship wars" that have plagued us, divided us, and driven us to make choices not based on the truth. I aim to be broadly ecumenical in these ideas but located in the "Free Church" worship tradition—a tradition with no set liturgy or prescribed prayers, no particular order or *ordo*—that may or may not draw from the traditions and practices of the larger church. Free Church worship may be wildly different from church to church, from plain and earnest worship in a small white clapboard building to the high worship one might call "Anglo-Baptist." So, as I wrote, the audience uppermost in my mind was part of the Free Church tradition. But those of us formed by that tradition must ask, with all Christians, "What does authentic worship look like? What is 'biblical' worship? How best can we draw from the riches of the broader church around the world and through the centuries?"

While seeking to be ecumenical in reach and spirit, this book is inevitably a personal offering—it comes from my own experience as a pastor and cellist, from all that has been given to me through the years, and from my love for many and varied worship traditions. I am neither a theologian nor liturgist by profession; I am rather a local church minister who sees the value of both theology and liturgy and seeks to offer their riches to the worship practices of God's people.

I hope this book will be accessible and adaptive to churches of all "styles" and "tastes" of worship and worship traditions, even those beyond the range of my worship and music experience. So take heart and courage, and may God bless the work of your holy imagination as you seek to serve the particular spiritual needs of your community of faith. Many days during the writing of this book, it became for me not only a book on worship, but also a book of worship. I pray that it will be an opportunity for worship for you as well.

Geoffrey Wainwright, in *Doxology: The Praise of God in Worship, Doctrine, and Life*, writes a systematic theology from a liturgical perspective.[3] He revives discussion of an old Latin phrase concerning worship, *lex orandi, lex credendi*, or the rule of prayer and the rule of faith. Does the rule of prayer establish the rule of faith, or does doctrine determine the practice of prayer and worship? Is one of them primary to the other? Wainwright writes from the creative interplay of the two, beginning with the liturgical life of the church. I believe, and my experience suggests, that faith and prayer flow out of each other. Worship is about the praise of God in mind, heart, and life. "Liturgy" is, as the Latin word means, *the work of the people*, and so in this book it refers to all the elements of a service of worship, words, and music. I have come to think of this book as pastoral theology from a liturgical perspective.

Over the centuries, various reform movements have sought to return worship to its biblical roots. But what exactly are those roots? As we survey the Bible, we find a songbook in the Psalms. We find a vision of worship given from Isaiah in the temple in Jerusalem where he saw the Lord high and lifted up—a vision in which we see confession, calling, and sending, all of them elements of true worship. We find glimpses of early church worship in Acts and Paul's epistles, and then, at the end of it all, worship in heaven in the visions of Revelation.

We also find the pivotal conversation between Jesus and the Samaritan woman at the well, which became a discussion of how best to worship: like the Samaritans on Mt. Gerizim or in Jerusalem as the Jews worshiped? Jesus transcended the first-century arguments over proper worship (early worship wars) with his answer, "God is spirit, and those who worship must worship in spirit and truth." (John 4:24).

That is what we all want: to worship in spirit and truth. How do we open ourselves to the Spirit in worship, and how do we worship in truth with as much as we can know of who God is, who we are, and what God wants, bringing ourselves as fully and truly as possible to God in worship?

These kinds of questions have occupied me in the writing of this book. I've divided the book into five sections.

Part One, "The Meaning and History of Christian Worship," examines the meaning of Christian worship and its long and complex history from its beginnings to the present.

Part Two, "An Order of Worship—Theological and Spiritual Reflections," offers a detailed examination of the "order of the liturgy," the movement of the people of God in worship from the Entrance and Gathering at the beginning of worship to the Sending Forth, Benediction, and Blessing at the end.

Part Three, "The Calling of Music in the Worship of God," discusses the sacred role of music in worship in its many different expressions, including psalms, hymns, spiritual songs, anthems, solos, and instrumental music.

Part Four, "Issues in Worship Today," considers some of the current issues in our desire to lead congregations in worship, such as inclusive language and worship that helps us bring our whole selves to God. This part also discusses the connection between worship and the moral life.

Part Five, "The Spiritual Practice of Planning and Leading Worship," offers practical guidance for weekly and long-term worship planning and considers the importance of the Revised Common Lectionary and the Christian Year.

The conclusion surveys our current landscape: "Living Water and Broken Cisterns—Toward the Renewal of the Church in the Renewal of Worship."

It is my deep desire that this book will spark conversation between ministers and church musicians, between ministers and church musicians with their congregation and in theological classrooms. I also hope it can aid worship boards and committees as they serve the worship of the church and provide a resource for congregational study. An Appendix provides various resources for worship as introduced in the body of the book.

Award-winning writer Annie Dillard, a psalmist and exegete of Creation, writes, "You were made and set here to give voice to this, your own astonishment."[4] This book on Christian worship is the voice of my astonishment.

Notes

1. Andre Dubus, "A Father's Story," in *The Times Are Never So Bad* (Boston: David R. Godine, 1983), 165.

2. George A. Buttrick, *Prayer* (New York: Abingdon Press, 1942), 83.

3. Geoffrey Wainwright, preface to *Doxology: The Praise of God in Worship, Doctrine, and Life; A Systematic Theology* (New York: Oxford University Press, 1980).

4. Annie Dillard, *The Writing Life* (New York: Harper & Row, Publishers, 1989), 68.

An Autobiographical Account of a Love of God and Love of Worship

In one sense I have been writing this book all my life. Growing up as a son of a Southern Baptist Minister of Music, I was immersed in music and worship. They were my mother tongue or at least my second language. Before my fourth-grade year, my parents took me to a music store to pick out the instrument I would play in the beginning fourth-grade orchestra. I tried several, but when I picked up the cello and drew a few timid sounds across the strings, I knew that was the instrument for me. As a cellist, then, I have always had a keen interest in the place of music in all forms of worship. The words of Abraham Heschel speak deeply to me and for me:

> In no other act does man experience so often a disparity between the desire for expression and the means of expression as in prayer. The inadequacy of the means at our disposal appears so tangible, so tragic, that one feels it a grace to be able to give oneself up to music, to a tone, to a chant. The wave of a song carries the soul to heights which utterable meanings can never reach. Such abandonment is no escape. . . . For the world of unutterable meanings is nursery of the soul, the cradle of all our ideas. It is not an escape but a return to one's origins.[1]

It is not only music that carries our souls; there are words too, the utterable ones we say and sing in worship. At their best they are a form of poetry. As I grew up singing in my father's choirs from childhood to college age, I learned to love the poetry of the songs, hymns, and anthems and to sing texts *as* poetry. This experience saved me from the literalism and fundamentalism of my Southern Baptist religion. The words in worship and song pointed beyond themselves to the ineffable.

I sang anthems from all genres and eras of sacred music; I sang gospel hymns whose refrains let you put down the hymnal, sing by memory, and be transported beyond the words: "Love lifted me . . . ." I sang the hymnody of the church throughout the centuries. Occasionally, I would play the cello in worship to accompany the choir or in a solo to express in sound what I could not express in words.

From those beginnings, I traveled to Stetson University, where I began as a cello major. Two years later, after sensing a call to ministry, I changed my major to religion. The music and worship at Stetson Chapel services transported me. After Stetson, I made my way to Union Theological Seminary in New York City, where I not only studied worship in classes but also experienced it in the extraordinary offerings of the great churches in the city. Riverside Church was next door, and St. John the Divine Cathedral was ten short blocks down Broadway.

As a pastor, I have served a small farming community church in Kentucky called Richland Baptist Church, a nineteenth-century white one-room schoolhouse kind of church building with two outhouses in the back. It had sometime during the years lost the steeple with the cross. One Sunday, people began noticing honey running down the plaster walls of the church from beehives inside the walls, an almost dream-like scene that reflected the richness of life in that place, its people and land. Its worship reflected traditional rural Southern Baptist worship. When a mouse ran across the floor, one of the youth was happily designated to pick it up by the tail and quietly carry it out of the church.

My first full-time pastorate was at a middle-sized congregation in Asheville, North Carolina, Beverly Hills Baptist Church, with people in the middle-class range of income and profession, with worship and music that was standard for moderate Southern Baptist churches at the time, and with an occasional rousing gospel piano solo by a member who was a host of a local gospel radio program.

My next church was Crescent Hill Baptist Church in Louisville, Kentucky, next to The Southern Baptist Theological Seminary. It was blessed with an extraordinary music and worship tradition aided by the students and professors and graduates of that seminary. Crescent Hill was on the vanguard of Baptist churches exploring and incorporating the riches of the worship traditions and practices of the broader ecumenical church.

Then I moved to a large center-city church in Ft. Worth, Texas, which was also enriched in worship and music by students, professors, and graduates of Southwestern Baptist Theological Seminary. Its worship and sacred music program were extraordinary, and while there, we built one of the most notable new organs in the world.

Next, I traveled to Myers Park Baptist Church in Charlotte, North Carolina, a large progressive church now associated with American Baptist Churches, USA. Its tradition of worship and music was shaped through the years by exceptional pastors, music ministers, and accomplished lay leaders. The church's first hymnal was the Presbyterian hymnal of the day, and then they created their own hymnal, a marvelous collection of hymns ancient and new.

Now I am serving my last church, Grace Baptist Church, a beloved, progressive, ministry-centered community of faith. It has around 100 members, and its worship and music serve the congregation beautifully.

These churches and my colleagues in each one have been my teachers in the meaning and practice of Christian worship. I could not write this book without them.

My worship life beyond my weekly pastoral calling has taken me to worship with the Benedictines at St. John's Abbey, Collegeville, Minnesota and Gethsemani Abbey near Bardstown, Kentucky. I have worshipped many summers at the Iona Abbey off the coast of Scotland. Led by the Wild Goose Resource Group, worship on Iona combines Scottish and World Christian music and liturgy. I've spent Sundays at St. Paul Baptist Church in Charlotte, worship that included the call-and-response Black music tradition. I've worshiped for an extended time at the Eucharistic services of Word and Table at St. Peter's Episcopal Church in Charlotte and also at Charlotte's Caldwell Presbyterian Church, remarkable for its lovely mix of races, sexualities, and incomes and its mission to the poor. I've worshiped at Pentecostal camp meeting services and at a Billy Graham Crusade. And I have experienced the grace of God in all of them.

Broadway Baptist Church gave me an enduring highlight of my worship life. Every Thursday, we hosted a weekly Agape Meal for the homeless population of Ft. Worth. We and our homeless guests, about 100 to 150 of them, ate a wonderful meal together, served home-style around the tables. We became friends. After the meal, we took a break, giving those who did not wish to stay for worship the freedom to leave (most stayed). Then together we worshiped around the dinner tables in what I thought of as "Corinthian Worship," worship like what Paul writes about in Corinthians, where we were all invited to bring a song, a prayer, a word, a witness as led by the Spirit (see 1 Cor 14:26). One night, a Hispanic man came to the front and sang his song to Jesus. The only word I recognized was *Señor*, or Lord, but it was unmistakably a love song to his Lord. Another night, a man suffering from schizophrenia and trying to stay on his meds played a jazz-like prelude. After the meal and worship, all were invited to Communion in the adjoining chapel. Some came with tears running down their faces. When you lose your home, you lose your church and its sacraments. They came like hungry birds to God.

One evening, a Hispanic man came for Communion. As he received the bread and cup, he crossed himself. I could almost sense him trembling. After the service, we talked and he thanked me. I said chattily, "The food is good here, isn't it?" He said, pointing to the table, "This is why I come."

I am an unabashed lover of worship in its beautiful panoply of forms. Some might say I am of profligate or indiscriminating tastes, but what is true worship but that which helps us taste and see that God is good? Any style that brings our whole selves into the presence of God is worthy worship.

I write this book on worship seeking to offer the best guidance I can after studying, planning, and leading worship for more than five decades. There have been moments of almost comical blunders, yet they were joined by moments when I have been, to use Charles Wesley's words, "lost in wonder, love, and praise."

Someone has said that all writing is autobiographical. So this book reflects a lifetime of worship experiences and study of worship, and yet it is but a thimble full of the ocean of the universal worship of the Holy One of the world.

Note

1. Abraham J. Heschel, *I Asked for Wonder: A Spiritual Anthology*, ed. Samuel H. Dresner (New York: Crossroad, 1983), 32–33.

Part 1

The Meaning and History of Christian Worship

Phrases like Worship Service or Service of Worship are tautologies. To worship God MEANS to serve him. Basically, there are two ways to do it. One way is to do things for him that he needs to have done—run errands for him, carry messages for him, fight on his side, feed his lambs, and so on. The other way is to do things for him that you need to do—sing songs for him, create beautiful things for him, give things up for him, tell him what's on your mind and heart, in general rejoice in him and make a fool of yourself for him the way lovers have always made fools of themselves for the one they love.[1]

Note

1. Frederick Buechner, *Wishful Thinking: A Theological ABC* (New York: Harper & Row, 1973), 97–98.

Chapter 1

The Meaning of Christian Worship

Worship is the submission of all our nature to God. It is the quickening of conscience by his holiness; the nourishment of mind with its truth; the purifying of the imagination by his beauty; the opening of the heart to his love; the surrender of will to his purpose—and all this gathered up in adoration, the most selfless emotion of which our nature is capable and therefore the chief remedy of that self-centeredness which is our original sin and the source of actual sin.[1]

It would be hard to find a more complete description of the meaning and purpose of worship than this one by Anglican theologian William Temple. I have seen the truth of this description at work in all three Abrahamic religions. In his book *Doxology*, Geoffrey Wainwright offers us his own definition of true worship: "Worship is . . . the concentration at which the whole of the Christian life comes to ritual focus."[2]

What then are the elements of true worship? British mystic theologian Evelyn Underhill comes to our aid. She lists four. The first is Ritual, a pattern of action that weaves the story of redemption into a sacred drama. Ritual transforms speech, gesture, song, and prayer into a design of worship that helps the worshiper "unite his physical, mental, and emotional being into a single response to the Unseen."

The second is Symbol. Symbols, Underhill writes, "signify, mediate, or suggest, but never explain the Reality that we adore." They are, in her words, "a sensible means of grace."

The third is Sacrament. The difference between symbols and sacraments is that a symbol "represents" while a sacrament "conveys":

"water cleanses, bread and wine feed, the oil anoints." In short, in the sacraments, God is acting, not just the worshiper. One might call worship a "Meeting Place." God has promised to meet us here.

The fourth element of worship is Sacrifice, and here we slow down. Underhill writes,

> Worship, the response of the human creature to the Divine, is summed up in sacrifice. . . . Its essence is something given, not given up. It is a freewill offering, a humble gesture which embodies and expresses . . . the living heart of religion, the self-giving of the creature to its God. By this self-giving action, man takes his conscious part in the response of the universe to the Source of its being; and unites the small movements of his childish soul to the eternal sacrifice of the Son.[3]

We can identify other key patterns of true worship. One is revelation and response. This happens throughout the service of worship. The encounter in the temple when Isaiah sees the Lord, "high and lifted up," provides a model for us: first the vision of the Lord, then the response of adoration by the seraphim around the throne. Next comes the confession wrenched from Isaiah's heart as he sees the holiness of God: "Woe is me! I am lost, for I am a man of unclean lips, and I live among a people of unclean lips"(Isa 6:5). Then comes the cleansing of his lips by one of the seraphim. Finally, there is the call of God to Isaiah to be God's prophet, followed by Isaiah's response: "Here am I; send me!" (v. 8).

These elements can be present in any form of Christian worship, from Pentecostal Holiness worship to Anglican worship at St. Paul's Cathedral in London, from the plain earnestness of rural Baptist worship to High Mass at St. Peter's in Rome and the worship at First Presbyterian in Pittsburgh, Pennsylvania. We worship in wooden pews and folding chairs; we worship surrounded by stained-glass windows or standing on beige linoleum floors. We worship in words carefully chosen and in words that flow out of the free expression of heart.

In terms of the practice of worship, I am led by Søren Kierkegaard's seminal depiction of Christian worship as a kind of theatre, but with roles reversed from cultural expectations. In his book *Purity of Heart Is to Will One Thing*, he says that when we go to the theatre, there are the actors on stage, the audience in the seats, and the prompter off stage, reminding the actor of his or her lines as needed. We are apt to see the worship leaders as the actors on stage, the worshipers as the audience, and God as the prompter. But this is all wrong, he says. In true worship, God is the audience, the worshipers are the actors, and the worship leaders are the prompters helping the worshipers say their right lines to God. And by right lines, I mean the words we most need to say to God, songs we most need to sing, prayers we most need to pray, both spoken and unspoken—the cries and whispers of our hearts.[4]

The implications of this insight, this new model of worship, are enormous. Yes, God is the first and truest audience, the center of our focus in worship. And yes, the work of worship is primarily the work of the congregation. They are the primary actors. And as for the leaders of worship, they are not saying their own lines in an individual and idiosyncratically personal sense. To do so turns the congregation into mere observers of the leaders' spirituality. Rather, worship leaders use prayers, songs, litanies and sermons universal enough in their spirituality that the people can hear and see themselves in it. The leaders in worship are not the prima donnas of worship but servants of the people of God, helping them come to the altar of God's grace, led by prayers, words, songs, and sermons. They are not the performers on stage but the prompters. For example, as I will discuss later, public prayer is not private prayer made public; it is prayer that helps the people of God pray as they most need to pray.

One could rightly say that the human creature is by nature a worshiping creature, *homo adoramus*. Archaeological evidence is in ample supply. We cannot help ourselves! We worship every day, in church and out, in the sanctuaries built by our human hands and in the great unroofed church of God in the beauty of God's creation. The psalmist says, "worship the LORD in the beauty of holiness" (Ps 96:9, KJV). Worship partakes of the beauty of God, of life, in the holiness of beauty, too. Annie Dillard writes, "I know only enough of God to want to worship him, by any means ready to hand." So along with walking in and out of Tinker Creek, she goes to the "one church here" on an island in Puget Sound, a small white-frame Congregationalist church where about twenty show up for worship. "Often," she writes, "I am the only person under sixty, and feel as though I'm on an archaeological dig of Soviet Russia."[5] But she goes, and so do we, in our own chosen or called places of worship.

We, however, cannot worship solely on our own. We need one another, not only those who worship with us on Sunday but also the great cloud of witnesses who have been helping us worship through the centuries (see Heb 12:1). An agnostic Jew was asked why he went to the Shabbat service since he did not believe. He answered, "I go to sit by my friend Saul; he believes."

True worship leads us away from the worship of the blinding, beautiful objects that tempt our devotion—distractions that are everywhere at every moment like wealth, status, physical beauty, and countless more. On and on they parade. The lure of glittering idols is strong, and worship helps break their hold on us. As John Calvin said, the human heart is a perpetual idol factory, so every week we go to worship to help break, iconoclastically, our false worship of the things we can see and touch and hold.

The disciples asked Jesus, "Lord, teach us to pray" (Luke 11:1). So we ask, "Lord, teach us to worship." We need the help of God and the presence of the Spirit every week. To paraphrase Paul, we know not how to worship as we want. We need the guidance of those who have worshiped through the centuries of our faith. And we need one another, for we worship more truly and honestly with others as their faith kindles, informs, and sustains our faith.

The words of the seventeenth-century parson and master poet of the English language, George Herbert, sum up my own heart as I begin this book on worship:

> King of glory, King of peace, I will love thee;
> and that love may never cease, I will move thee.
>
> Thou hast granted my request, Thou hast heard me;
> Thou didst note my working breast, Thou hast spar'd me.

Wherefore with my utmost art I will sing thee,
and the cream of all my heart I will bring thee.

. . .

Sev'n whole days, not one in seven, I will praise thee;
In my heart, though not in heaven, I can raise thee;

. . .

Small it is, in this poor sort to enroll thee;
Ev'n eternity is too short to extol thee.[6]

Notes

1. William Temple, *Nature, Man and God* (n.p., 1949) quoted in *The Oxford Book of Prayer*, ed. George Appleton (Oxford: Oxford University Press,1985), 3.

2. Geoffrey Wainwright, *Doxology* (New York: Oxford University Press, 1980), 8.

3. Evelyn Underhill, *Worship* (London: Nisbet & Company, 1936), 32–49.

4. Søren Kierkegaard, *Purity of Heart Is to Will One Thing* (New York: Harper Brothers, 1938), 160–66.

5. Annie Dillard, *Holy the Firm* (New York: Harper & Row, Publishers, 1977), 55, 57.

6. George Herbert "King of Glory, King of Peace, Praise (II)," in *George Herbert: Country Parson and the Temple*, ed. John N. Wall Jr. (New York: Paulist Press, 1861), 270–271.

Chapter 2

A Short History of Christian Worship with an Emphasis on Free Church Worship

Sometimes the present can free us from the shackles of the past and help us build the future. But sometimes something from the past can free us from the shackles of the present and help us build the future. —Fred Turner[1]

The idea of writing a one-chapter history of Christian worship reminded me of a play I once attended, *The Complete Works of William Shakespeare (Abridged)*, that compressed all of Shakespeare's plays into one ninety-minute show! It was a whirlwind and great fun, so rather than attempt an exhaustive (and exhausting!) history, we'll frame the epic story of Christian worship as a play. Take your seats as the show begins.

Act 1: *Early Church Worship as Glimpsed in the New Testament*

The earliest followers of Jesus continued to worship in the temple and in synagogues. As Luke writes with the last words of his Gospel, "And they worshiped him and returned to Jerusalem with great joy, and they were continually in the temple blessing God (Luke 24:52-53). They also worshiped in the synagogue through Hebrew Scripture, prayers, explications on the readings, and songs.

We get a glimpse of synagogue worship of that time in Luke 4:16-30 when Jesus returns to Nazareth and gives his inaugural sermon based on the reading from Isaiah. The text tells us that his sermon incited a riot, and he was carried out of the synagogue to be thrown off a cliff. It is a sober reminder of the transformative power and sometimes danger of worship and preaching.

At some point in the mid-first century, the synagogue and the emerging church experienced a painful divorce. Synagogue services at the time included a set of benedictions and maledictions, and at some point, the maledictions began to include those who followed Jesus as Messiah. When the Jesus followers would not join in the malediction, they were cast out of the synagogue (see John 9:22 and 9:34). Premier New Testament scholar J. Louis Martyn locates the schism as happening before John's Gospel was written.[2]

For a while in the New Testament period, Christians worshiped as Jews on the Sabbath and then met again on Sunday for an Agape meal and Communion. After the break with the synagogue, Sunday worship became normative. We see this pattern described by Paul in 1 Corinthians 11, and the book of Acts adds to our understanding of early worship practice in Jerusalem: "They devoted themselves to the apostles' teaching and fellowship, to the breaking of bread and the prayers" (Acts 2:42).

These four areas of devotion—teaching, fellowship, Communion, and prayer—set the tone of their worship and their life together. Even as they still worshiped in the temple, "day by day, . . . they broke bread at home and ate their food with glad and generous hearts, praising God and having the goodwill of all the people" (Acts 2:46-47).

First Corinthians shows that early Christian worship was a combination of the ecstatic and the rational. Believers sang and prayed "in the Spirit" and also prayed and sang "with the mind." Paul's writing also offers a glimpse of how participatory and free the worship was: "What should be done then, my brothers and sisters? When you come together, each one has a hymn, a lesson, a revelation, a tongue, or an interpretation" (1 Cor 14:26). The only guidelines of such participatory worship were that "all things be done for building up" the whole Body of Christ.

Early Christian worship borrowed prayers, Scripture, and songs from the synagogue and then added the Service of the Table. From that time, the two essential elements of worship have been the Service of the Word and the Service of the Table. As we cover the history of Christian worship, we shall learn about eras when one or the other of these two elements was emphasized, sometimes to the neglect of the other.

Act 2: Worship in the Early Centuries

The earliest written record of Christian worship comes from the second century, dated c. 150 CE and written by Justin Martyr. When we examine it, we see both comparisons and contrasts with worship forms today:

> And on the day called Sunday, all who live in cities or in the country gather together to one place, and the memories of the apostles or the writings of the prophets are read, as long as time permits; then when the reader has ceased, the president verbally instructs, and exhorts to the imitation of these good things. Then we all rise together and pray, and . . . when our prayer is ended, bread and wine are brought, and the president in like manner offers prayers and thanksgivings, according to his ability, and the people assent by saying Amen; and there is a distribution to each, and a participation of that over which thanks have been given, and to those who are absent a portion is sent by the deacons. And they who are well to do, and willing, give what each thinks fit; and what is collected is deposited with the president, who succours the orphans and widows, and those who, through sickness or any other cause, are in want, and those who are in bonds, and the strangers sojourning among us, and in a word takes care of all who are in need. But Sunday is the day on which we all hold common assembly, because it is the first day on which God, having wrought a change in the darkness and matter, made the world; and Jesus Christ our Saviour on the same day rose from the dead.[3]

We see in Justin Martyr's account these basic elements that comprise much of worship today:

Gathering on the Lord's Day, Sunday
The Service of the Word
Prayers of the Congregation
The Service of the Table
The Offering
The Dismissal (This includes the taking of Communion to those not present and the giving of alms to those in need, seeking to follow the command of Jesus in Matthew 25:35-36.)

Today, there is a new emphasis in scholarship on the varieties of belief and worship in what is called "Early Christianities"—plural! There was variety in worship as Christian communities arose in diverse places like Rome, Egypt, Corinth, and Syria. Paul Bradshaw argues for the "pluriformity" of early Christian worship.[4] Michael Hawn makes use of Bradshaw's scholarship as he invites us to open ourselves to "world music" coming from every continent and culture. Hawn's book, *Gather into One: Praying and Singing Globally*, is a rich and eye-opening resource for the church today.[5]

Act 3: Medieval Worship

Next came the emergence of the two main branches of Christianity, the Eastern Orthodox Church and the Roman Catholic Church, each developing its own worship traditions.

Three key terms describe Eastern Orthodox worship: Mystery, Beauty, and the Divine Presence. As Geoffrey Wainwright observes, "The point, in Orthodox terms, is that worship is first and foremost the 'presence and act of God.'"[6] In the Eucharist the Divine Presence fills the whole sanctuary, present not just in bread and wine. Preserving the Mystery of God, an iconostasis, a wall of icons, partly hides the congregation from the actions of the priests. Beauty in all its forms dwells in the sanctuary, received by all the senses. Icons help worshipers gaze upon the beauty of the Lord. Incense fills the air as the fragrance of the Lord, and there is the taste of the bread and wine of the Eucharist. Architectural beauty suggests the beauty of the Cosmos with God as the Sovereign of the world. In worship, the worshiper dwells in community not only with those present but also with all the saints throughout history. The Greek Orthodox theology of salvation focuses on the Incarnation and our partaking of the divine nature, called divinization. Second Peter 1:4 is a central verse of Scripture for Eastern Orthodox worshipers, as evidenced in the ancient prayer of the people as they approach the "Divine Mysteries": "The Divine Body both deifies and nourishes me; it edifies my soul and strangely nourishes my mind." Reverence for the early tradition of worship has meant that Orthodox worship has remained virtually unchanged from the earliest years until now.

The other branch of Medieval Christianity, the Roman Catholic Church, made the Eucharist the center of worship. This branch's theology of salvation, which was centered on the atonement of the cross and human sinfulness, created the form of the Mass that focused on the Sacrifice of Christ and our participation in it. In the Roman Catholic Church of this period, preaching became less a part of Medieval worship.

Dom Gregory Dix's magisterial work, *The Shape of the Liturgy*, notes that in the Medieval period, the Mass was something "said" and "heard," with the priests doing the saying and the congregation hearing and watching. He draws a contrast, stressing that worship is something we "do," not something we "say." From the early periods of worship, worship was something we did! In the Medieval period, there was the "saying of the Mass," but in the early Christian period, worshipers were described as "doing the eucharist" or "performing the mysteries."[7]

Evelyn Underhill writes of the "catholicity," that is, the comprehensive range of Roman Catholic worship. Using the words of Karl Adam in his *The Spirit of Catholicism*, she notes,

> Catholicism is the result of . . . baptizing into Christ all the religious longings and religious desires of men. It can therefore absorb, and carry forward, many differing levels and strands of worship; can offer a home to the crudest products of popular religion, yet can also introduce the contemplative to the "wilder-

ness where lovers lose themselves"; gathering all into its "great supra-national tidal wave of faith in God and love of Christ."[8]

It was this wideness of spirit—with both its glory and weakness—that fueled the Reformation's aim: to purify the worship and theology of the Church and return to the origins of Christian worship in the Bible.

Act 4: Reformation Worship

The Reformation was a radical reconstruction of both theology and worship. As the leaders of the Reformation reworked their theology, they also underwent a reformation of worship practice. The prophetic dimension of worship, that is, preaching, was restored to a place of prominence.

Martin Luther represents the most conservative wing of Reformation worship. He promoted the least change in the Mass. The theological meaning of the Eucharist was changed, but its basic form remained the same. Luther, however, led the reemergence of the important balance of the Service of the Word and the Service of the Table in worship.

In contrast to Lutheran restraint in changes to worship, the Anabaptists and Quakers formed a radical left wing, while John Calvin and Reformed Church worship formed a middle way. Calvin stripped the Mass of its ceremonial and sacramental character and elevated the preaching office. Like Luther, he wanted a return to the balance of the Service of the Word and the Service of the Table in Sunday worship. The magistrates in Geneva, however, stipulated a quarterly observance of the Lord's Table. Swiss reformer Ulrich Zwingli argued for the purely symbolic nature of the Eucharist and moved the altar out of the sanctuary, replacing it with a common movable table that stayed to the side except when Communion was observed.

On the left wing of the Reformation, the Anabaptists wanted worship to contain only elements described in the Bible. Their worship was spare and featured preaching and the involvement of the congregation all the way through. Its order consisted of:

Prayer
Scripture
Prayer
Sermon
Congregational Interpretation of the Texts
Prayer
Offering

The Society of Friends, or Quakers, moved the farthest from the sacramentalism and clericalism of the established church. They did away with sacraments and priests altogether. One described their worship as "the quiet gathering of souls together to share fellowship with God."[9]

The English Reformation found its center in the Anglican Church and *The Book of Common Prayer*, a spiritual and liturgical masterpiece. It sought a middle way between Rome and Calvinist worship, aiming to preserve the liturgical tradition of the Western Church and to restore the centrality the Eucharist in Sunday worship.

Act 5: Free Church Worship from Its Beginnings Until Today

The term "Free Church" involves two dimensions of the word "free." The first is freedom from the constraints of a nationally established church, such as the Anglican Church in England; the second is freedom from the set prayers and worship of the Anglican and Roman Catholic liturgies.

Those who opposed a national church in England and elsewhere were called variously Separatists, Nonconformists, and Independents. From this group arose, among others, Presbyterians, Congregationalists, and Baptists.

Free Church worship could be anti-liturgical, or it could retain a liturgical format for worship. It could reject set prayers, prescribed or not, in favor of spontaneous and improvised prayer, or it could use prayers written for church worship. Churches favoring a liturgical order most often adopted and adapted what is called "The Genevan

Order," which is still the foundation of Presbyterian worship. The 2003 Presbyterian *Book of Common Worship* recommends this order of Sunday worship:

THE GATHERING
    Call to Worship
    Prayer of the Day, or Opening Prayer
    Hymn of Praise, Psalm, or Spiritual
    Confession and Pardon
    The Peace
    Canticle, Psalm, Hymn, or Spiritual
THE WORD
    Prayer for Illumination
    First Reading
    Psalm
    Second Reading
    Anthem, Hymn, Psalm, Canticle, or Spiritual
    Gospel Reading
    Sermon
    Hymn, Canticle, Psalm, or Spiritual
    Affirmation of Faith
    Prayers of the People
    Offering
THE TABLE
    Invitation to the Lord's Table
    Great Thanksgiving
    Lord's Prayer
    Breaking of the Bread
    The Communion
SENDING
    Hymn, Spiritual, Canticle, or Psalm
    Charge and Blessing[10]

When we look at the worship of the non-liturgical Free Churches, we see a wide variety in worship style and worship order. The early Regular Baptists (non-Calvinist in theology) had a worship form close to that of the Anabaptists. Their service was simple with prayers, psalms, Scripture, the sermon—followed by three or four laypeople adding their interpretations of the text—and an offering for the poor. The Lord's Supper was celebrated in an afternoon or evening service. In the eighteenth century, the Regular Baptists established a monthly celebration of the Lord's Supper in morning worship.[11]

A Traditional Baptist Order in the revivalist tradition (sometimes called in Southern Baptist life the "Sandy Creek" Tradition) might look like this:

Hymns
Prayer
Welcome and Announcements
Special Music (choir, solo, or small group)
Offering
Solo
Sermon
Invitation and Invitation Hymn
Benediction

In the more formal Baptist tradition (sometimes called the "Charleston" Tradition), we might see this order:

Prelude
Welcome and Announcements
Invocation
Hymn of Praise
Morning Prayer
Scripture
Offertory
Anthem
Sermon
Hymn of Invitation or Dedication
Prayer and Benediction
Postlude[12]

In progressive Baptist worship life today, we might see something close to the Genevan order:

Welcome and Announcements
Prelude
Choral Call to Worship
Invocation
Hymn of Praise
Confession
Organ Voluntary
Scripture(s)
Anthem
Sermon
Prayers
Offertory
(Communion on Communion Sundays, often once a month)
Hymn of Dedication
Benediction
Postlude

So we see that the leaders of Free Church worship have an almost dizzying array of resources from which to choose—to use an Anglican phrase, "an embarrassment of riches." The breadth and freedom of Free Church worship may cause those who plan and lead such worship to suffer a kind of agoraphobia—the fear of wide-open places—since we have so much from which to choose. The good news is that we have so much from which to choose!

The End

Sometimes at the end of a play, the playwright or director appears onstage with a final word to the audience. So now I appear onstage with these words:

Thank you for attending this play. I hope it has been helpful and edifying and not too arduous! As we have watched the major players and movements through the history of Christian worship, key questions and tensions have arisen over and over again. Shall we have the Eucharist every Sunday? Is the Service of the Word and Service of the Table a prerequisite for Christian worship? Is worship primarily something heard and watched by the worshipers? Or is it something *done* by the congregation? Shall there be a set form for the liturgy and prayers or a freer form with extemporaneous prayers? Is there freedom in worship for the Spirit to move, for example, in the different kinds of Spirit-led worship of Pentecostals and Quakers?

Amid these modern questions, through all the centuries until now, the second-century worship described by Justin Martyr has continued to guide the worship of the church: Prayers, Song, Scripture, Sermon, the Table of Our Lord, and an Offering taken for the poor and the needs of the world. The styles and forms of worship change and oscillate. They evolve and sometimes go back to the beginning and start all over again!

And yet "worship in spirit and truth" (John 4:24) has by the grace of God been our Meeting Place with the Divine somewhere in all places and times. God is not a perfectionist about worship. God comes to welcome us, delight in us, guide us, and abide with us in the multitudinous ways we seek best to worship the Living One.

An Interlude: Convergence in Worship Today and a Representative Worship Order

Singing is at home in the liturgy because worship bears, in Christianity as in other religions, the character of dromenon, *a complex drama of words and actions in which music may help to bring mental and physical activity together in unity or in counterpoint.*[13]

Today, we are fortunate witnesses of a "convergence" in the study and practice of Christian worship. Spurred on by the Ecumenical Movement and its quest for unity in the church and in the elements of worship we share across denominational lines, we see a movement toward union in reconciled Christian diversity.

In 1982, the World Council of Churches met in Lima, Peru, to explore the growing agreement and remaining differences among its members. One of the excellent papers published, "The Baptism, Eucharist and Ministry (Faith and Order Paper no. 111, the 'Lima Text')" was a major achievement and remains a valuable reference in matters of agreement between churches.[14]

As mentioned in the previous chapter, there is also a new appreciation of the historical and modern "pluriform" nature of Christian worship. From the first century until now, we see a worldwide beautiful diversity of worship. Yet amid this diversity, it may also be fruitful to look closely and deeply at one converging worship order as a way to help us plan worship no matter what tradition is our home. Perhaps a close examination of this order may invite the gift of holy improvisation or reveal new ways of helping the worship of the people of God within your own tradition's form and order of worship.

An order of worship based on this new convergence might look like this:

The Gathering or Entrance Rite

> Prelude
> Greeting
>> Introit
>> Processional Hymn
> Opening Prayers
>> Collect or Invocation
>>> The Confession of the People of God and Assurance of Pardon

The Service of the Word

> Old Testament Lesson
> New Testament Reading
> Psalm
> Gospel Reading
> The Hymn or Anthem
> The Sermon

The Affirmation of Faith
The Prayers of the People
The Offertory (the Bringing of Gifts for Ministry and for the Table
on Sundays when Communion or Eucharist is celebrated)
The Doxology
The Prayer of Dedication

The Service of the Table

The Prayer of Thanksgiving
The Words of Institution with the breaking of the bread and
pouring of the cup
The Prayer of Consecration
The Serving of Bread and Cup
The Sharing of the Peace

The Sending Forth

The Hymn of Dedication/Recessional Hymn
The Charge to the People of God
The Benediction and Blessing
The Postlude

Now as we begin Part 2, let us take this order as a template that
will guide us to think deeply about each movement of public worship.
Each element of the worship service is vital to the whole. And each
element is an act of a drama, as it begins in Entrance and Gathering
and ends in the Sending, Benediction, and Blessing.

Notes

1. Frederick Turner, "Art Recentered: A Manifesto" *Frederick Turner's Blog: Mark My Words*, https://frederickturnerpoet.com/?page_id=99.

2. J. Louis Martyn, *History and Theology in the Fourth Gospel* (Nashville: Abingdon Press,1968), 37–62.

3. Roberts, Alexander, James Donaldson, and Arthur Cleveland Cox, *The Ante-Nicene Fathers: Translations of the Writings of the Fathers Down to A.D. 325; The Apostolic Fathers with Justin Martyr and Irenaeus*, vol. 1 (Eugene, OR: Wipf and Stock Publishers, 2022), 186.

4. Paul F. Bradshaw, *The Search for The Origins of Christian Worship* (New York: Oxford University Press, 1992).

5. C. Michael Hawn, *Gather into One: Praying and Singing Globally* (Grand Rapids: Eerdmans Publishing Company, 2003).

6. Geoffrey Wainwright, *Doxology* (New York: Oxford University Press, 1980), 242.

7. Dom Gregory Dix, *The Shape of the Liturgy* (Glasgow: The University Press, 1945), 12.

8. Evelyn Underhill, *Worship* (London: Nisbet & Company, 1936), 246.

9. Underhill, *Worship*, 308.

10. *Book of Common Worship* (Louisville, KY: Westminster John Knox, 1993), 46.

11. See the entries of Thomas Halbrooks, *Twenty Centuries of Christian Worship*, vol. 2 (Nashville: Star Song Publishing Group, 1994), 82–83, 231–35.

12. See Donald P. Hustad, "Non-Liturgical Churches—Revivalist vs. 'Formal Evangelical Worship," in *Jubilate: Church Music in the Evangelical Tradition* (Hope Publishing Company, 1981), especially 116–119.

13. Wainwright, *Doxology*, 199.

14. "Baptism, Eucharist and Ministry," *Faith and Order*, no. 111 (Geneva: World Council of Churches, 1982), https://www.oikoumene.org/resources/documents/baptism-eucharist-and-ministry-faith-and-order-paper-no-111-the-lima-text.

Part 2

An Order of the Worship of God—Theological and Spiritual Reflections

Chapter 3

Entrance and Gathering

Early in the morning our song shall rise to Thee. —Reginald Heber

One summer afternoon, I was traveling down a rural road in Ashe County, North Carolina. I rounded a curve and saw, on a green hill, a beautiful frame church, painted a weathered white. The sign in front gave its name: "Sabbath Welcome Baptist Church." I've driven that road many times since, and my heart is captured every time. The name comes from an old tradition of having a Sabbath Welcome Service on Saturday evening before Sunday worship. I confess that I have often longed for such a service. How often I—we—could use an evening service that would prepare us for the next day's Sabbath.

But that is not our tradition, and our Sabbath mornings most often go something like this:

The alarm rings, and you drag yourself out of bed. It's Sunday morning, and you're going to church. You make a cup of coffee and perhaps glance at the news. It may be the quietest morning of the week. Or maybe not. If you live in a family with children, soon they will be jostled out of bed, despite their protests— "Do I have to?!" With or without children, the Sunday morning ritual of getting your household fed, showered, and dressed in time for church may strain the emotional equilibrium.

You get in your car. If you have children with you, there may be a quarrel or two from the back seat. If you are alone, you may have a quarrel or two inside your head.

Sunday morning may be the time you feel most like a minority as a churchgoing Christian. Where is everybody? The streets are quieter than usual. You may pass people in restaurants and parks and wish you were among them. You may be running late. You may have had a strong disagreement the night before. You may be worried about the world, your family, your nation. You might not feel well, but you are on the way to church. There may be a lingering residue of regret, guilt, or shame.

But there is something else there, however buried: your hunger for God. The psalmist's cry is your own:

> As a deer longs for flowing streams,
> so my soul longs for you, O God.
> My soul thirsts for God, for the living God.
> When shall I come and behold the face of God? (Ps 42:1-2

In ancient times, Hebrew people sang the Psalms of Ascent as they climbed the holy hill to Jerusalem and the temple. These psalms had words like "I was glad when they said to me, 'Let us go to the house of the LORD!'" (122:1). Under all your other thoughts and feelings, you share the gladness of climbing toward a place of worship.

You drive into the church parking lot. You are here by a miracle, the miracle of gathering. God has brought you here. But you might not yet be ready to worship. How could you be? You need the first act, the first movement of worship, Entrance and Gathering.

Samuel Miller, former dean of Harvard Divinity School and pastor of Old Cambridge Baptist Church, wrote a book titled *The Life of the Church*. In it, he tells the story of Abbot Robert of Molesme, founder of the Cistercian Order. When the Abbot went to the chapel, he would stand at the door and wait in silence before he opened it and entered the chapel space. As his monks watched, they learned the importance of what he was doing and began to follow him in this spiritual practice. They too put their hand on the knob of the door and waited. In Miller's words, "They refrained from haste while they prepared to enter into the presence of the everlasting God."[1]

Having arrived at church, we need help slowing down from the haste of the world and preparing to worship. What are we hungering and thirsting for as we enter? What troubles do we bring to God, and what hope do we bring?

Our entrance into the church is both a Pilgrimage and a Preparation. If we enter first into an anteroom or narthex, we may see a baptismal font. We may touch our fingers to the water, then to our foreheads, and remember, "I am baptized."

Or we may enter a busy, noisy foyer with bright conversation and greetings. Either way, we are moving from secular space and time to sacred space and time in which worship may happen. It is a practice as ancient as time, the sacred movement of the body into a place of worship.

We take our seats in the sanctuary, maybe holding a bulletin that was given to us as we entered. We hear music, an organ or piano or musical ensemble, escorting us in sound from the secular to a sacred hour of worship. Some call this moment of entering into the sacred the Introit. I have in my home an abstract piece of art by Joseph Albers. Called *Introit*, it is composed of a set of long lines that form brilliant yellow rectangles, one inside the other, radiating from large to small like an endless doorway. Here at the Introit, we are leaving the world and entering a door, a holy space, a space "set aside," made holy by our intention.

From ancient times and in many religious traditions, a bell or other sound centers our attention in this moment. In some churches a bell is rung three times, in Trinitarian pattern, called the Angelus.

The service begins. Often, the minister or priest starts with a biblical greeting and blessing, "The Lord be with you," and we respond, "And also with you." Or "And with your spirit." In some churches, the minister and congregation exchange a "Good morning," a mutual greeting in the name of God. Whatever words are offered, this call and response is the first of many such moments in worship. It is the first blessing of worship. Keith Watkins describes three purposes of the Entrance Rite:

1. It brings the people together and constitutes them as a congregation.
2. It declares the theological foundation of what is happening.
3. It is the congregation's first address to God.[2]

And now Gathering has happened. The people of God are reminded of who they are, the people of God, and why they are here. We are "re-membered" into the Body of Christ.

There should be joy in this first movement of the worship service. Mark's Gospel tells a story of this kind of joy. Jesus and his disciples are leaving Jericho and pass a blind man named Bartimaeus. Bartimaeus cannot see, but he hears the bustle and commotion and cries out, "Jesus, Son of David, have mercy on me!" The man's cry stops Jesus in his tracks, and Jesus says to his disciples. "Call him here." The disciples run to Bartimaeus, saying the glad words that call us all into worship: "Take heart; get up, he is calling you." (Mark 10:46-49)

Yes, he is calling us. And so we sing:

> Brethren, we have met to worship and adore the Lord our God;
> will you pray with all your power, while we try to preach the Word?
> All is vain unless the Spirit of the Holy One comes down:
> Brethren, pray and holy manna will be showered all around.
>
> Sisters, will you join and help us? Moses' sister aided him;
> will you help with trembling mourners who are struggling hard with sin?
> Tell them all about the Savior—tell them that he will be found:
> Sisters, pray and holy manna will be showered all around.[3]

The first prayers of worship are prayers of Invoking and Beseeching. British poet T. S. Eliot watched as the sun set on the seventeenth-century chapel of Little Gidding. Moved, he wrote,

> You are not here to verify,
> Instruct yourself, or inform curiosity
> Or carry report. You are here to kneel
> Where prayer has been valid.

And it begins, he adds,

> By the purification of the motive
> in the ground of our beseeching.[4]

With the Invocation we pray for the Holy Spirit to draw near and open us to the presence of God. Long ago, before it was known as the Invocation, it was called the *Epiclesis*, the calling down of the Holy Spirit. Hippolytus, in his Apostolic Tradition, dated around 200 CE, prayed what became the model Epiclesis:

> We entreat you to send your Holy Spirit upon the offering of the holy church. Gather into one all who share in these holy mysteries, filling the Holy Spirit and confirming their faith in the truth, that together we may praise you and give glory through your servant, Jesus Christ.

Historically, the Epiclesis been used most often in the prayers offered at the Eucharist, but in whatever form, it is important to pray it at the beginning of worship. Thus we begin worship by beseeching the Spirit's presence in every moment of worship. The Collect from the *Book of Common Prayer* guides us well:

> Almighty God, unto whom all hearts are open, all desires known, and from whom no secrets are hid: Cleanse the thoughts of our hearts by the inspiration of thy Holy Spirit, that we may perfectly love thee and magnify thy holy Name; Through Jesus Christ our Lord.

It is true that we could call every prayer at every moment in worship an Epiclesis. "Come, Holy Spirit, Come" is our active, breathing prayer throughout our service of worship. With Paul, we rely on the help of the Spirit from the beginning of worship, before any prayer can even be uttered: "Likewise the Spirit helps us in our weakness, for we do not know how to pray as we ought, but that very Spirit intercedes with groanings too deep for words" (Rom 8:26). We call on the Spirit with the prayer of Illumination before the reading and preaching of Scripture: "Let the words of my mouth and the meditation of my heart be acceptable to you, O LORD, my rock and my redeemer" (Ps 19:14). We call on the Spirit in the prayer before the Table:

Gracious God,
Pour out your Holy Spirit upon us
and upon these your gifts of bread and wine,
that the bread we break
and the cup we bless
may be the communion of the body and blood of Christ.
By your Spirit make us one with Christ,
that we may be one with all who share this feast,
united in ministry everyplace . . . .[5]

Finally, we beseech the Spirit to go with us in the sending forth and
benediction: "The grace of the Lord Jesus Christ, the love of God,
and the communion of the Holy Spirit be with all of you" (2 Cor
13:13).

All these prayers and all our actions begin in the prayer of
Beseeching that opens our worship. Having gathered, entered
together into a sacred hour, and prayed for the Spirit of God to be
present with us, we are ready for the second movement in worship:
Praising, Blessing, Thanking, Awe, and Delight.

Notes

1. Samuel H. Miller, *The Life of the Church* (New York: Harper and Brothers, 1953), 27.

2. Keith Watkins, *The Great Thanksgiving: The Eucharistic Norm of Christian Worship* (St. Louis: Chalice Press, 1995).

3. "Brethren, We Have Met to Worship," in *The Worshiping Church Hymnal* (Carol Stream, IL: 1990), Hymn 802. Words attributed to George Askins, 19th century. Tune: HOLY MANNA.

4. T. S. Eliot, "Little Gidding," in *Four Quartets* (New York: A Harvest Book/Harcourt, Inc., 1971), 50, 57.

5. *Book of Common Worship* (Louisville, KY: Westminster John Knox, 1993). 129

Chapter 4

Praising, Blessing, Thanking, Awe, and Delight

It is very meet and right that we should give thanks unto thee; that we should adore, glorify, laud, exalt, honour, hymn with praises, bless and sanctify the one majesty of the Holy Trinity. —Early Syrian preface to worship

The first major movement in worship is Adoration. Adoration seems like a word from the past, but let us resurrect it. It includes praising, blessing, thanking, awe, and delight. Thankful praise is the dominant spirit of Christian worship. Our Jewish roots made *barakah*, blessing the Lord, a key element of worship. The Greek word *Eucharisto*, which means both grace and thanks, not only underlines the meaning of the Eucharist but also speaks to the heart of worship.

The opening hymn of the worship service often begins our praise. Hymnal pages spill over with plenteous hymns of praise, and in them we find praise to God the Creator, Sustainer, Provider, Redeemer, and Friend. "Praise to the Lord, the Almighty, the King of Creation."[1]

Praise has many voices. There is expressive praise, like the rhythmic joy that allows our bodies to get into the act: O clap your hands! Hallelujah! Praise Yahweh! O sing unto the Lord a new song. There is contemplative praise as we ponder in quieter tones, "Why do I love thee, O God?" Lutheran pastor Jaroslav Vajda's hymn is a moving example:

God of the sparrow, God of the whale,
God of the swirling stars.
How does the creature say Awe
How does the creature say Praise?[2]

Jane Marshall's anthem, "My Eternal King," begins in contemplative praise, using the words of a seventeenth-century Latin text, translated by Edward Caswell:

My God I love thee;
not because I hope for heav'n thereby.
Nor yet because who love thee not must die eternally.
Thou, O my Jesus, Thou didst me upon the cross embrace.

Then Marshall ends her anthem in exultant praise:

Why, then, why, O blessed Jesus Christ,
Should I not love Thee well,
Not for the hope of winning heav'n,
Or of escaping hell;
Not seeking a reward;
But as Thyself has loved me, O ever-loving Lord!
E'en so, I love thee, and will love,
And in thy praise will sing;
Solely because Thou Art my God,
And my Eternal King.[3]

Hymns and songs of thanksgiving pervade the beginning of worship. If praise is the expression of love for who God is, thanksgiving offers gratitude for what God has done and is doing. Our hymns give voice to this endless thanksgiving, as in the anthem setting of E. E. Cummings's poem "i thank you God" that celebrates the goodness of God in the world and ends in a cascade of "thank you and thank you." The familiar hymn setting of the words of St. Francis brings all creation and all creatures into the praise of God. "All Creatures of our God and King," the hymn begins, then sun and moon, rushing wind, flowing water, and sailing clouds join the song.[4]

Jesus's whole life was characterized by gratitude. When he said in the Sermon on the Mount, "Consider the lilies" and "Look at the birds of the sky," it was more than a lesson about the good provision of God. Jesus was exulting in the wildflower-strewn hillsides of his boyhood Galilee and the beauty of birds arrayed as God's own royalty and whose songs were the perfect praise of God. Even when he realized the tide had turned against him and that rejection and death lay ahead, he prayed, "I thank you, Father, Lord of heaven and earth, because you have hidden these things from the wise and the intelligent and have revealed them to infants; yes, Father, for such was your gracious will" (Matt 11:25-26). In everything, as Paul urged, we should give thanks (see 1 Thess 5:18).

But there is awe too, and this first act of worship is filled with awe, for we worship a holy God whose ways are not our ways and whose thoughts are not our thoughts. God is God and we are not. We sing the words of the seraphim as they flew around the throne of God in Jerusalem's temple when Isaiah saw the Lord high and lifted up, "Holy, Holy, Holy" (Isa 6:1). In the presence of the holy, we may feel, like Isaiah, "undone." In the Old Testament, a predominant image of God's holiness is fire. When God encountered Moses in the burning bush, Moses took off his shoes, for he knew this was holy ground. God's fire purifies and cleanses but does not destroy. Here are the words of St. Symeon, The New Theologian (c. 1000 CE):

Rejoicing, at once trembling,
I who am straw receive the fire
And, strange wonder!
I ineffably refreshed
As the bush of old
Which burned yet was not consumed.

Awe and wonder are our responses to God in worship. We may find awe to be a forgotten element in our worship and missing in our lives too, like a forgotten vestige from the past, but it is essential to our spiritual, physical, and mental health. Psychologist Dacher Keltner describes awe as "a feeling of being in the presence of something so vast that it transcends your understanding of the world."[5] A sense of awe may come as we look up at the millions of stars in the sky. Or it may come when we see an act of moral courage, an act of surprising kindness, or attend the birth of a child. Wonder, too, is a part of our worship. Rabbi Abraham Heschel, in an oft-quoted passage, writes,

> Our goal should be to live life in radical amazement . . . get up in the morning and look at the world in a way that takes nothing for granted. Everything is phenomenal; everything is incredible, never treat life casually. To be spiritual is to be amazed.

How does our own worship evoke awe and wonder when our secular age confines everything in the horizontal frame? Something beyond us, some transcendence, is lost. Worship bids us to leave the secular enclosures of our mind and world, to go outside and look up. What tools do we have to aid us? We can use the poetry of awe and wonder in worship, an often-unexpected resource. Poetry slows us down and helps us see. Here are the words of poet Sidney Lanier, not only looking at the "Marshes of Glynn" but "seeing" them:

> Behold I will build me a nest on the greatness of God:
> I will fly in the greatness of God as the marsh-hen flies,
> In the freedom that that fills all the space 'twixt marsh and the skies,
> By so many roots as the marsh-grass sends in the sod
> I will heartily lay me a-hold of the greatness of God.[6]

Our poets can lead us; they are our liturgists of awe, praise, and wonder. They strike the hour of awe.

Now we turn to Delight. Should there not be an element of delight in worship? God takes delight in us and in what God has made, and this God, our God, wants us to enter into pleasure and delight in worship. When do we experience delight in worship? How can we make room for it? In some congregations, the people dance with delight in God and God's delight in us. In other churches, delight comes as a complete surprise! The Shakers made dance a central part of their life together, and their most recognized hymn expresses delight as they danced in their circle dances:

'Tis a gift to be simple, 'tis a gift to be free,
'Tis a gift to come down to where we ought to be;
And when we find ourselves in the place just right,
'Twill be in the valley of love and delight.[7]

What brings delight to our minds and hearts in worship? Music and poetry can. The presence of children never fails to bring delight. In some of the churches I served, the smaller children began the service sitting at the front of the sanctuary on the floor. At the singing of the first hymn, they made their happy way out, clambering and skipping down the aisles. The congregation enjoyed shared delight in the goodness of God to bring children to us.

I have often celebrated the dedication of infants and children in this early movement of worship. I would carry the child in my arms, walk them down the aisle, and introduce them to their family of faith. I would offer a blessing to the child, like God's original blessing to us all, and the people in the pews would feel vicariously their own original blessing from God. Praise, thanksgiving, wonder, awe, and delight, all in the welcome of a child.

When Jesus was baptized, God's voice from heaven said, "This is my Son, the Beloved, with whom I am well pleased" (Matt 3:17). Can we believe that God takes delight in us? At the heart of Jesus's spirituality was his experience of God as *Abba*, his God who took delight in him, a relationship of intimacy, confidence, trust, and obedience.

A priest from Belfast was visiting his uncle in Ireland. It was his uncle's eightieth birthday. One morning before dawn, they went for a walk along Lake Killarney. As they stood side by side watching the glorious sunrise, his uncle began skipping down the road, radiant. The nephew caught up and said, "Uncle, you look really happy." His uncle replied, "I am lad. . . . You see, me Abba is very fond of me!"[8] Our God is very fond of us. In the Westminster Brief Catechism, perhaps the most well-known question is "What is the chief end of man?" And the answer is "The chief end of man is to glorify God and to enjoy him forever." The enjoyment—can we believe it?—goes both ways.

Wendell Berry writes, "In the right sort of economy our pleasure. . . would be both an empowerment of work, and its indispensable measure. Pleasure. . . perfects work." [9] We who plan worship can bear this in mind as we approach our own work. If those planning public worship feel pleasure in its planning and creation, the people may feel pleasure in worship too.

Delight often arrives when we encounter the happy unexpected. And what could be more unexpected in worship than play? My planning team and I have occasionally created worship services that have an element of play about them. One such service was inspired by a book, *14,000 Things to Be Happy About.*[10] The worshipers were handed crayons and blank sheets of paper along with their bulletins as they entered the sanctuary. During the sermon I invited them all, children and adults, to draw or write things that make them happy, things that are indeed part of God's salvation as blessing. Then we shared what we had drawn and gave thanks and praise to God.

The poet Denise Levertov writes of the importance of the poetry of anguish, anger, and rage as we experience the cruelty and injustice of the world. But then she goes on:

> We need also the poetry of praise, of love for the world. . . . A passionate love of life must be quickened if we are to find the energy to stop the accelerating tumble . . . toward annihilation. To sing awe—to breath out praise and celebration—is as fundamental an impulse as lament.[11]

So let us breathe out praise and celebration! In them we come alive.

We have begun in praise, blessing, thanksgiving, awe, and delight. Now we move to what in many worship traditions is the next movement of worship, Lament and Confession.

Notes

1. Joachim Neander, "Praise to the Lord, the Almighty," 1680, trans. Catherine Winkworth, 1863, tune: LOBE DEN HERREN, https://hymnary.org/text/ praise_to_the_lord_the_almighty_the_king.

2. Jaroslav J. Vajda, "God of the Sparrow, God of the Whale" (GIA Publications, 1983).

3. Sam Hodges, "'My Eternal King' launched top Methodist composer," *UM News*, July 9, 2014, https://www.umnews.org/en/news/ my-eternal-king-launched-top-methodist-composer.

4. St. Francis of Assisi, "All Creatures of our God and King," 1225, tune: LASST UNS ERFREUEN, https://hymnary.org/text/all_creatures_of_our_god_and_king.

5. Dacher Keltner, *Awe, The Transformative Power of Everyday Wonder*, quoted in Hope Reece, "How a Bit of Awe Can Improve Your Health," *The New York Times*, January 3, 2023.

6. Sidney Lanier, "The Marshes of Glynn," in *Hymns of the Marshes*, public domain.

7. Joseph Brackett, "Simple Gifts," in *Ritual Song*, 2nd ed., #856.

8. Brennan Manning, *Abba's Child: The Cry of the Heart for Intimate Belonging* (Colorado Springs: NavPress, 1994), 65.

9. Wendell Berry, "The Profit in Work's Pleasure," *Harper's Magazine*, March 1988, 21.

10. Barbara Ann Kipfer, *14,000 Things to Be Happy About: Newly Revised and Updated* (1990; repr., n.p.: Workman Publishing Co., 2014).

11. Denise Levertov, "Poetry, Prophesy, Survival," in *New and Selected Essays* (New York: A New Directions Book, 1965), 144.

Chapter 5

Lamentation and Confession

Life is completely fair. It breaks everybody's heart. —Anton Myrer[1]

There is a gap between what ought to be and what is, between what we yearn for in ourselves and for the world and what is. Worship that is of spirit and truth includes the need for lament and confession. This is the movement of the undefended self. We live such defended lives, spending so much energy defending ourselves to ourselves and justifying ourselves to others. Now in worship, we let our Defense Department go and bring our real selves before God, our true selves, or as much of our true selves as we can know. If true worship is the bringing of the whole self to God, lament and confession are a requisite part.

Mystic theologian Evelyn Underhill writes,

> . . . the essence of purification is self-simplification; the doing away of the unnecessary and unreal . . . purity is an affirmative state; something strong, clean and crystalline, capable of a wholeness of adjustment to the wholeness of a God-inhabited world.[2]

The movement of the worship service called Lament and Confession requires nothing less than this "self-simplification," a simplicity that lies on the far side of complexity. One Prayer of Confession begins,

> Gracious God,
> our sins are too heavy to carry,
> too real to hide,
> and too deep to undo.

Forgive what our lips tremble to name,
what our hearts can no longer bear . . .[3]

With such a prayer on our lips, true confession is possible. Acknowledging the truth about ourselves can bring relief and freedom.

As to lament, it need not be seen as the opposite of praise. Liturgical theologian Gail Ramshaw writes, ". . . just as praise opens the
door for lament, lament always turns back to praise."[4] Noted Brooklyn
preacher W. A. Jones tells of a conversation with a woman in the foyer
after church. He asked, "How are you today?" She replied, "Pastor,
I'm somewhere between 'Thank you, Jesus!' and 'Lord, have mercy!'"
Praise and lament intertwine. That's how our worship begins: praise,
lament, and back to praise.

The prophet Isaiah experienced God's presence in the temple,
a primal encounter that altered his life. After the seraphim praised
God's holiness and beauty, Isaiah lamented, "Woe is me! I am lost,
for I am a man of unclean lips, and I live among a people of unclean
lips" (6:5). It was a cry of spiritual distress. It was his confession, his
lament over his own condition, and also a cry for a world in distress
and sin. We experience such sadness over own sin, when we have
fallen short of our highest values, or when we are overcome by the
cruelty and violence of the world. We might even experience sadness
when we are in the presence of beauty and goodness that causes us to
see dimness of our own lives.

The book of Psalms is full of laments, though we tend to ignore
them in worship. John Calvin called Psalms "the anatomy of all parts
of the soul." Having preached the Psalms, I agree. "My God, my
God, why have you forsaken me?" the psalmist cries in Psalm 22:1,
a cry of desolation that Jesus repeated on the cross. David cries in
Psalm 51: "my sin is ever before me. . . . Create in me a clean heart,
O God" (vv. 3, 10). In Psalm 94:3, the psalmist cries out, "How long
shall the wicked, how long shall the wicked exult?" With the psalm-
ists, we bring our sadness and the sadness of the world to God, for we
cannot escape "how sad and bad and mad" the world, to use Robert
Browning's phrase.

There once were a number of laments in our hymnbooks, hymns that brought our sorrow and sadness to God, both personal lament and lamentation for the world:

Come ye disconsolate, where-e'er you languish
Come to the mercy seat, fervently kneel;
Here bring your wounded hearts, here tell your anguish:
Earth has no sorrow that heav'n cannot heal.[5]

I've observed over the years that such hymns seem to have been grad-ually excised from most hymnals. The ones closest to lament that we of the Baptist tradition may still sing include "I Need Thee Every Hour" and "What a Friend We Have in Jesus." This elimination of songs of sorrow does not seem to be as prevalent in Black Church worship. The Black Church's bandwidth for both joyful praise and deep lament is wider than that of other churches. For generations, Black spirituals have voiced human brokenness and the brokenness of the world. "I must walk this lonesome valley, I got to walk it by myself," sings the first verse of one spiritual. Then, in the last verse, Jesus joins them: "Jesus walked this lonesome valley, he had to walk it by himself."[6] In this song, the anguish of the human soul is joined by the suffering Jesus.

I have known church growth experts who advised eliminating such songs, saying, "Confession is a downer. Hymns in a minor key are a downer! Avoid them." How, then, are the people of God to worship when life becomes a "downer"? Where shall the people of God find communion in suffering if these songs are banished from our worship? Songs about sorrow, eliminated from our hymnbooks, still find a welcome in folk music, country music, and the blues, like Joan Baez's "Where Have All the Flowers Gone?" Or Hank Williams's "I'm So Lonesome, I Could Cry." Black theologian James Cone called the blues "secular spirituals," like this one:

Times is so tough, I can't even get a dime,
Yes, times is so tough, can't even get a dime.
Times don't get better, I'm going to lose my mind.

One blues singer sings,

> blues ain't nothin
> But a poor man's heart disease.[7]

If lamentation is part of what we must pour out to God, so is confession. We come confessing because we trust that there is a God whose forgiveness is already flowing to us and whose help is on the way. The church, through the centuries, has created prayers of confession to help give us words that help express our confessions and the ways we have fallen short of God's moral demands and our own most treasured values.

I think there is significance in the congregational confession of sins. It breaks through what Richard Rohr has called "the cult of innocence" that exists in the church—and in our society as well. And I think it is important for young people to hear their elders pray such prayers. The young will learn soon enough about the sins of adults, and these prayers give them a head start on spiritual honesty.

I offer here three Prayers of Confession and the corresponding Declarations of Forgiveness—which is how lament turns back to praise. How, without the knowledge of forgiveness, could we risk such prayer?

From A *New Zealand Prayer Book* (Anglican):

> Almighty and merciful God,
> we have sinned against you,
> in thought, word and deed.
> We have not loved you with all our heart.
> We have not loved others
> as our Savior Christ loves us.
> We are truly sorry.
> In your mercy forgive what we have been,
> and help us to amend what we are,
> and direct what we shall be;
> that we may delight in your will

and walk in your ways,
through Jesus Christ our Savior. Amen.

Declaration of Pardon
Almighty God who pardons all who truly repent,
forgive your sins and strengthen you by the Holy Spirit,
and keep you in life eternal. Amen.[8]

From *The Iona Abbey Worship Book*:

Leader: Let us in silence confess our faults and admit our frailty.
All: Before God, with the people of God,
We confess to our brokenness:
To the ways we wound our lives,
The lives of others,
And the life of the world.

Declaration of Pardon
Leader: May God forgive you, Christ renew you,
and the Spirit enable you to grow in love.
All: Amen.

Then, because praise issues into lament and lament into praise, the
Iona Community follows with this Affirmation of Faith:

Leader: With the whole church
All: We affirm
That we are made in God's image,
Befriended by Christ, empowered by the Holy Spirit.
Leader: With people everywhere
All: We affirm
God's goodness at the heart of humanity,
Planted more deeply than all that is wrong.
Leader: With all creation
All: We celebrate
The miracle and wonder of life;
The unfolding purposes of God,
Forever at work in ourselves and in the world.[9]

From the *Book of Common Worship* (Presbyterian):

> Eternal God, our judge and our redeemer,
> we confess that we have tried to hide from you,
> for we have done wrong.
> We have lived for ourselves,
> and apart from you.
> We have turned from our neighbors,
> and refused to bear the burdens of others.
> We have ignored the pain of the world,
> and passed by the hungry, the poor, and the oppressed.
> In your great mercy forgive our sins
> and free us from selfishness,
> that we may choose your will
> and obey your commandments;
> through Jesus Christ our Savior.
>
> Declaration of Forgiveness
> The mercy of God is from everlasting to everlasting.
> I declare to you, in the name of Jesus Christ,
> you are forgiven.
>
> May the God of mercy,
> who forgives you all your sins,
> strengthen you in all goodness,
> and by the power of the Holy Spirit
> keep you in eternal life.
> Amen.[10]

I have had conversations with some who recoiled at congregational prayers of confession. "These aren't my sins," they've said. "Don't put these words in my mouth!" But, like Isaiah, we confess and we grieve not only our own sins but the sins of the church and of our nation, community, and world. We are dealing with reality, and wrongdoing is part of it. Evelyn Underhill defines mysticism as ". . . the art of union with Reality."[11] Lord, give us such art. Prayers of confession unite the reality of wrong with the reality of God's goodness.

Music can help evoke confession in this part of the service when words alone fail. And music can offer the grace of forgiveness in ways that reach deeply into the heart. I have witnessed such with the hymn of confession, "Dear Lord and Father of Mankind." Imagine how movingly a soloist singing the Black spiritual "Sometimes I Feel Like a Motherless Child" could highlight the sorrowing and suffering in the congregation.

God does not want lament to be your whole life, but when a lament is all you have to offer, God covets your honest cry. A rabbinic story is told of a young rabbinical student who left his hometown and went to the city to study with a rabbinical Master. One day he came to him and said, "Master, my life is in torment. Back home, everything was simple, everything was clear. I studied, I prayed. But now I cannot study, I cannot pray. I am in torment; everything is confused. I am lost. Please help me study and pray as before."

The rabbi paused and thought and said, "And who told you God wants your study and your prayers? Perhaps God prefers your suffering and your tears."

We might object, "No, God would never prefer suffering!" But if suffering and tears are all we have to offer to God, God wants us to bring them. Jesus might say, "What parent, if their child was suffering and hurting, would want them to suffer in silence alone?" Of course, a loving parent would want their child to come near and would listen to hear their small voice. "How much more, then," Jesus would say, "does your heavenly Abba want to hear your cries?"

Much of the world's sorrow does not come from sin but from what Miguel de Unamuno calls "the tragic sense of life." A car skids off the highway; lives are lost. An infection rages through a person's body, or a nation's whole body in a pandemic. A hurricane smashes into a town and sweeps lives away. In these moments, too, we cry out our laments. In his classic, *The Tragic Sense of Life*, Unamuno writes,

> . . . I am convinced that we should solve many things if we went into the streets and uncovered our griefs, which perhaps would prove to be but one sole common grief, and joined together in beweeping them and crying aloud to the heavens and calling upon

God. And this, even though God should hear us not; but He would hear us.

Then he offers these concluding words: "The chiefest sanctity of a temple is that it is a place to which men go to weep in common."[12] Unamuno was speaking of what he called "the Common Weeping." What a compounded tragedy it would be if our temples, our churches, our worship closed the door to those who need to weep in common.

Notes

1. Anton Myrer, *The Last Convertible* (New York: Putnam New York, 1979).

2. Evelyn Underhill, *Practical Mysticism: A Little Book for Normal People* (E.P. Dutton & Co., 1915), 36.

3. *Book of Common Worship* (Louisville, KY: Westminster John Knox, 1993), 88.

4. Gail Ramshaw, *Words that Sing* (Chicago: Liturgical Training Publications, 1992), 28.

5. "Come, Ye Disconsolate," in *African American Heritage Hymnal* (Chicago: GIA Publications, Inc., 2001), #421.

6. James H. Cone, *The Spirituals and the Blues: An Interpretation* (New York: The Seabury Press, 1972), 67.

7. Cone, *The Spirituals and the Blues*, 115.

8. *A New Zealand Prayer Book* (San Francisco: Harper San Francisco:1989), 37–38.

9. *The Iona Abbey Worship Book* (Iona Community: Wild Goose Publications, 2001), 16–18.

10. *Book of Common Worship*, 53, 56.

11. Underhill, *Practical Mysticism*, 3.

12. Miguel de Unamuno, *The Tragic Sense of Life* (New York: Dover Publications, 1954), 17.

Chapter 6

The Service of the Word—The Word of God Read and Proclaimed

The word of God
never comes to an end.
No word
is
God's last word. —Abraham Heschel[1]

The Service of the Word is more than the sermon. When I was growing up in the Southern Baptist tradition, the only Scripture read was the sermon text, and the minister read it. In many churches today, the reading of Scripture is unfortunately one of the most life-less moments in the service. But in the history of worship, the reading of Scripture was often elevated to a place equal to the sermon, and not one text alone but several texts were read, often with a psalm or anthem or canticle between the readings. In the Anglican/Episcopal tradition, after the reading of the Old Testament, Psalm, and Epistle, the priest carries the Bible into the congregation for the reading of the Gospel, with the congregation standing as the Gospel is read. It is one of the service's most important moments. I have worshiped in Episcopal services and felt the Word of God as it is read in the texts for the day wash over me, refreshing me.

We need a word from beyond ourselves, a wisdom deeper than our opinions, a Word from God; so, in worship, there is Scripture and there is the sermon. In some religions and religious traditions, the time of worship is wordless, sermon-less, but in Christian worship, in continuity with our Jewish antecedents, there is what we call "The Service of the Word."

Synagogue worship was formed after the destruction of the temple as the Hebrew people went into exile in Babylon. The synagogue service had these parts:

1. The Gathering
2. The Shema ("Hear O Israel" from Deuteronomy 6:4), sung or chanted
3. The Blessings
4. The Reading of the Torah
5. The Psalms, sung and or read
6. The Reading of the Prophets
7. A Sermon delivered sitting by the head of the synagogue or by someone invited to do so
8. The Benediction

In Judaism, there is the Written Torah and the Oral Torah, the latter being rabbinic commentary on the Five Books of Moses, which sets the stage for oral interpretation of Scripture at the synagogue service. As Abraham Heschel wrote, "No word is God's last word."

If worship is to be worship in both spirit and truth, the truth of Scripture must be read, interpreted, and proclaimed. The preacher must be as faithful to the Scripture as possible and be willing to tell the truth as best they know. It would be an apt addition to the Ordination Prayer and Charge for ministers to include: "Tell the truth!"

Sometimes the sermon comes, as the saying goes, to comfort the afflicted and at other times to afflict the comfortable. Such is true, for this is also what Scripture does. Sometimes, unfortunately, the preacher plays to the whims and prejudices of the congregation and culture. As Paul wrote to Timothy, "For the time is coming when people will not put up with sound teaching, but, having their ears tickled, they will accumulate for themselves teachers to suit their own desires" (2 Tim 4:3). There are plenty of preachers ready to tickle those ears, whether for false comfort or the easy condemnation of others. In the Old Testament, we see true and false prophets, some who speak the truth God has given them to say and some who speak what others want them to say, whether king or congregation.

"The word is near you, in your mouth and in your heart," Paul wrote (Rom 10:8). God's word is as near as our own breath, as close as the beating of our hearts, and yet sometimes we need the help of another person to hear it. During the madness of the Third Reich and the Reich Church, Dietrich Bonhoeffer helped form the Confessing Church and an underground seminary for pastors. In his book *Life Together*, he describes the daily worship of the community:

> Help must come from the outside, and it has come and comes daily and anew in the Word of Jesus Christ. . . . God has willed that we should seek and find His living Word in the witness of a brother [and sister], in the mouth of another, bringing redemption, righteousness, innocence, and blessedness. . . . Therefore the Christian needs another Christian who speaks God's Word to him [and her].[2]

God reveals God's self in many ways, but we must not neglect the central revelation of the Word of God in Scripture. The Hebrew Scripture for the Jewish community is composed of three parts: Torah, the Prophets, and the Writings (such as Job and the Psalms). Picture them as three concentric circles with Torah at the center, then around it the Prophets, and around it the Writings. The Jewish word for their Hebrew Scriptures, *Tanach*, is an acronym of the Hebrew letters of the three parts: *Torah, Nebiim,* and *Kethubim.* The synagogue offers readings from all three at every service.

The Christian New Testament adds a fourth circle to the Hebrew three circles, the *Euangelion*, or Gospel. Our best worship provides for the fullness of Scriptures: Old Testament, Psalms, Epistles, and Gospels, even if the sermon does not deal with all the readings. The Three-Year Revised Common Lectionary provides a regular way to use all dimensions of the Bible each Sunday.

God's word is alive in many ways. I love the Iona Community's responses after the reading of Scripture:

Leader: For the Word of God in scripture,
For the Word of God among us,
For the Word of God within us.
All: Thanks be to God.[3]

In this movement of worship, then, the Spirit of God seeks to bring together what has been sundered—the Word in Scripture and the Word within us. I once read a murder mystery in which a Native American says, "My uncle, he used to say there was two Bibles . . . . Or one, but it has been split in half. He said half's in the book, on paper. But the other half is inside people. You born with it."[4] The Service of the Word is about the Word of God in Scripture, reconnecting with the Word of God among us and within us.

In the book of Nehemiah, the prophet Ezra stands in the marketplace of Jerusalem and reads the Word of God. The people of Israel had just returned after their long exile in Babylon. It had been many years since those in the crowd had heard the Word of God publicly read; for some, it was the first time they had heard it read at all. Stepping onto a high wooden platform built in the midst of the city, Ezra began to read. Some of those gathered wept for joy to hear the Word, so long silent, read aloud. Others wept in remorse and guilt as they realized how far they had fallen from God's way. To them, the prophet said, "This day is holy to the LORD your God; do not mourn or weep. . . . Go your way, eat the fat and drink sweet wine . . . , for the joy of the LORD is your strength" (Neh 8:9-10). So we rightly say, after the reading of Scripture, "Thanks be to God!"

In many worship traditions, the Service of the Word includes a "Prayer of Illumination" not before the sermon but before the reading of the Scriptures. The United Methodist Book of Worship gives us this one:

Lord, open our hearts and minds
by the power of your Holy Spirit,
that, as the Scriptures are read
and your Word proclaimed,
we may hear with joy what you say to us today. Amen.[5]

A beautiful prayer of illumination handed down to me goes like this:

> O Lord, send your Holy Spirit
> that we may hear your Word,
> and hearing your Word, love your voice,
> and loving your voice, do your will. Amen.

Now we are ready for the preaching of the Word. Paul underlined the crucial nature of preaching:

> For "everyone who calls on the name of the Lord shall be saved."
> But how are they to call on one in whom they have not believed?
> And how are they to believe in one of whom they have never
> heard? And how are they to hear without someone to proclaim
> him? And how are they to proclaim him unless they are sent? As
> it is written, "How beautiful are the feet of those who bring good
> news!" (Rom 10:13-15)

The preacher is the servant of the Word. I was asked once how growing up as a cellist affected my preaching. First, I answered, it has taught me discipline. As the old joke goes, a man flagged down a cab in New York City and asked, "What is the way to Carnegie Hall?" The cabbie answered, "Practice, practice, practice!" A sermon is first offered to God, and a sermon worthy to offer to God demands the hard work necessary to listen to and proclaim the Word of God. But the second part of my answer was more important: being a cellist means becoming a servant of the manuscript of music. The manuscript tells you when to shout and when to dance, when to weep and when to whisper. All the markings are there. So the preacher reads the text as a manuscript of music.

Jesus told a parable about the wisdom of Scripture: "every scribe who has become a disciple in the kingdom of heaven is like the master of a household who brings out of his treasure what is new and what is old" (Matt 13:51-52). This is the hope we bring to the reading and proclamation of the Scriptures: treasure from the past and some new word for the current hour, the written word becoming new in our hearing and in our worship together.

There are many kinds of sermons, but I believe the kind of preaching most needed in worship is what I call "textual preaching," in which the minister chooses which of the scripture texts for the day will be the basis for the sermon. George Buttrick, one of the greatest preachers of the twentieth century, taught, "Choose the one that makes you salute!" In addition, I would add, we must seek the aid of the Holy Spirit and ask, "Which text best serves the needs of the congregation at this point in time?"

The basic unit for preaching is the scriptural paragraph, or *pericope*, the unit of verses most translations have already marked off. It may be a story, a psalm, or an ethical teaching. One verse is too little, giving too much latitude for the preacher to preach whatever is on his or her mind. Thirty verses may send the sermon flying off in all directions at once.

Biblical preaching also involves the integral rhythm of biblical narrative and the commands of God. Ancient rabbinic commentary on Scripture was of two kinds, *Halakah* and *Haggadah*. *Halakah* was the study of and commentary on the laws and commandments of God as revealed in Scripture and the application of them to daily living. *Haggadah* was the study and imaginative retelling of the narratives of Scripture. Old and new stories were woven together. If *Halakah* was their duty, *Haggadah* was their delight.[6] A faithful preacher brings both kinds of Scripture and both kinds of interpretation to the people of God.

The Bible itself displays the intrinsic, interwoven pattern of story passages and law passages. In Exodus, we see first the story of the emancipation of the Hebrew people from slavery in Egypt. Then in chapter 20, we see the giving of the Ten Commandments. Chapter 20 begins in verse 1, "I am the LORD your God, who brought you out of the land of Egypt, out of the house of slavery"; then God gives the commandments, ten of them. It is as if God were saying, "I set you free and brought you here. Now to *stay* free, 'you shall have no other gods before me. You shall not . . . You shall not . . . .'"

The Gospel of Matthew, as the new Five Books of Moses, is set up in the same sequence of story followed by teaching. The story of Jesus's birth and ministry begins with the gospel, and then comes the

Sermon on the Mount. Four more times in Matthew the stories of Jesus's ministry are followed by teaching passages, each of which ends with, "and when Jesus had finished saying these words . . . ."

Preachers may use the Revised Common Lectionary to find and use this pattern, or they may create their own series of sermons in a *lectio-continua* pattern, that is, by following a continuous set of texts over a number of weeks. For example, a series on Jesus's healings might be followed by a series on the Ten Commandments, or a series on Old Testament biblical figures might be followed by a series on the commands of Christ. The sermon is set in the midst of worship and preached to a community of believers who have been well prepared to hear it.

A last, perhaps most important word is "listen." This word begins the *Shema*, the central Hebrew creed: "*Shema Y'srael!*" Hear, O Israel! Israel and the church are people who stand before God and listen. The readers of Scripture in worship should take time to listen deeply to the text as they read, pausing where appropriate, enunciating clearly, and showing a reverence for the Word of God.

For those who preach, the listening begins on Monday as they open the Bible and read and spend time listening to God's Word before consulting any other book, commentary, or resource. As Dale Moody, one of my beloved professors, quipped, "The Bible throws a lot of light on the commentaries!"

In his *Tales of the Hasidim*, Martin Buber pictures how we proceed:

> I shall teach you the best way to say Torah. You must cease to be aware of yourselves. You must be nothing but an ear which hears what the universe of the word is constantly saying within you. The moment you start listening to what you yourself are saying, you must stop.[7]

We listen, we pray, and then, tremblingly, we speak.

Notes

1. Abraham J. Heschel, *I Asked for Wonder* (New York: Crossroad, 1981), 85.

2. Dietrich Bonhoeffer, *Life Together* (New York: Harper and Row, 1954), 22-3.

3. *The Iona Abbey Worship Book* (Iona Community: Wild Goose Publications, 2001), 18.

4. Sara Gran, *Claire DeWitt and the City of the Dead* (New York: Houghton Mifflin Harcourt, 2011), 96.

5. *The United Methodist Book of Worship* (Nashville: The United Methodist Publishing House, 1992), 34.

6. My development of this rabbinic tradition is in my book. H. Stephen Shoemaker, introduction to *GodStories: Scriptural Narratives from Sacred Texts* (Valley Forge, Pennsylvania: Judson Press, 1998), xvi, x.

7. Martin Buber, *Tales of The Hasidim: The Early Masters* (New York: Schocken Press, 1947), 107.

The Affirmation of Faith

. . . we both believe and disbelieve a hundred times an Hour, which keeps Believing nimble. —Emily Dickinson

Some days we may agree with Emily Dickinson: "we both believe and disbelieve a hundred times an hour." We might further agree that in our day, we need to keep "believing nimble." Harvey Cox writes in *The Future of Faith* that the Spirit of God is causing an upheaval that is "shaking and renewing" Christianity. "Faith," he writes, "rather than beliefs, is once again becoming [Christianity's] defining quality, and this reclaims what faith meant during its early years."[1]

Karen Armstrong makes a similar argument in her book *The Case for God*. She says that faith at its deepest level is captured in words like "trust," "confidence," "loyalty," and "engagement." These words are the language of personal relation.[2] It is more a believing *in* than a believing *that*, though the second can serve to moor one's faith. When I was young, I sang a Scripture song based on 2 Timothy 1:12: "I know whom I have believed . . . ." Not What, but *Whom*. As William Sloane Coffin writes in his book *Credo*, "Credo—best translates 'I have given my heart to.'"[3]

We might say that the crucial question of our faith is not "What do I *have* to believe?" but "What do I *need* to believe?" What do I need to believe in order better to live my life as a follower of Jesus? What do I need to believe in order to be the person God made me to be and the person I most want to be, to be able to withstand the onslaughts and challenges of life, to survive life's shipwrecks and setbacks? What do I need to believe in order to live with confidence, clarity, and strong faith? Our creeds, personal, congregational, and denominational, grow from the answers to these questions. Martin Luther rose every morning with his personal creed on his lips: "I am baptized!" Some mornings I need to rise from my bed and say, from the Apostle's Creed, "I believe in the forgiveness of sins!" It might save my day.

As important as they have been in the history of the church, creeds have less credence today. Sometimes creeds have become the enforcers of what it means to be a Christian. Worse, creeds have been used to justify the persecution of "heretics," those of "unstraight faith," by the "orthodox," those of "straight faith." Sometimes the enforcers want to be "theological orthodontists," there to straighten out our faith. But "orthodoxy" literally means "straight praise" or "right praise" or "right worship." It's about how to worship God truly. When the sword of the State is placed in the hands of heresy hunters, terrible things like the Inquisition happen. Indeed, on February 27, 380 CE, Emperor Theodosius I issued an edict enforcing allegiance to the Nicene Creed and forbidding any change or deviation from it at the pain of both "temporal and eternal punishment." When State and Church get in bed together, the Church had best keep its eyes open through the night. Rowan Williams, former Archbishop of Canterbury reflected on orthodoxy and heresy, writing that we need "to experience orthodoxy as something still future," not fixed perfectly for all time.[4]

Despite their misuse, our creeds can and do provide a healthy dimension to our faith. In his provocatively titled book, *Not Every Spirit: A Dogmatics of Christian Disbelief*, theologian Christopher Morse reflects on "faithful disbelief." Sometimes we need to faithfully reconsider what we believe. Yet he also writes of the importance of the doctrines of the church, saying that they are like "buoys that mark the channels of the deep": "They neither contain nor confine the depths, but they point their direction by warning of the shallows." Our communal doctrines are "buoy-markers of the mysteries of God known to faith."[5]

We need creeds and affirmations of faith that go beyond personal faith and beliefs to the faith and beliefs of the church. Our personal faith can become wobbly, our hearts fluttering this way and that. In those times, we need the sturdy structure of creeds and statements of faith in worship that reaffirm our faith when it is insecure. At church, we help each other believe, not just by the recitation of belief but by our very presence together. As Paul wrote to the church in Rome, "For I long to see you so that I may share with you some spiritual gift so that you may be strengthened—or rather so that we may be mutually encouraged by each other's faith, both yours and mine" (Rom 1:11-12).

We need to participate in the faith of the church. In many worship traditions, the congregation recites a historic creed or other affirmation of faith after the sermon. "We believe . . . ," the congregation begins, and they voice the faith of the church. From its beginnings, Christian worship has been, by its nature, a corporate experience, and at this moment of worship, the body corporate expresses its faith.

In non-creedal churches, an affirmation of faith written by the denomination or the local congregation is often read. The Presbyterian *Book of Common Worship* has a "narrative creed" that tells the story of the faith and the story of Jesus. It fills in the space between "born of the Virgin Mary and "suffered under Pontius Pilate," a space left open in many creeds. Here is its beginning:

> In life and in death we belong to God.
> Through the grace of our Lord Jesus Christ,
> the love of God,
> and the communion of the Holy Spirit,
> we trust in the one triune God, the Holy One of Israel,
> whom alone we worship and serve.

Note that to this point the word *trust* is used rather than *believe*. Next comes the part of the creed that is about Jesus:

> We trust in Jesus Christ,
> fully human, fully God.
> Jesus proclaimed the reign of God:
> preaching good news to the poor
> and release to the captives,

teaching by word and deed
and blessing the children,
healing the sick
and binding up the brokenhearted,
eating with outcasts,
forgiving sinners,
and calling all to repent and believe in the gospel.
Unjustly condemned for blasphemy and sedition,
Jesus was crucified
suffering the depths of human pain
and giving his life for the world.
God raised Jesus from the dead,
vindicating his sinless life,
breaking the power of sin and evil,
delivering us from death to life eternal.

Then there follows, in classical trinitarian form, sections on God, "We trust in God . . . ," and then on the Holy Spirit, "We trust in the Holy Spirit . . . ."[6]

In an earlier chapter I offered an affirmation of faith used by the Iona Community in its worship. The Iona Community places that affirmation right after the Confession and Assurance of Pardon. A non-creedal church may wish to do the same.

There are special Sundays in the Christian Year where an affirmation of faith may fit that day of worship. For example, here is an Affirmation of Faith used widely for Palm Sunday, placed after the sermon:

We believe that the man who rode into Jerusalem on a donkey
is the Lord of all history and of every day.
We believe he came to save us from our sin,
and to restore us to God.
We believe he was cruelly treated,
that he was put to death on the cross,
and then buried in a borrowed tomb.
We believe that God raised him from the dead,
and that he became the first fruits of those who were asleep.
We believe that he is present in our midst today,

comforting our sorrow,
showing us the way to tomorrow,
and challenging us to life in the kingdom.
We believe that the day will come
when the entire world will be reconciled and Christ will reign in
glory
as the Redeemer of all that was separated from God,
receiving our praise forever and ever. Amen.

Affirmations of faith help the congregation affirm together
the beliefs that help sustain their lives. This is a grace of corporate
worship, that we encourage and build up each other's faith as we
worship together—a practice that goes back to the days of the early
church. Paul wrote to Timothy,

> I am reminded of your sincere faith, a faith that lived first in your
> grandmother Lois and your mother Eunice and now, I am sure,
> lives in you. For this reason I remind you to rekindle the gift of
> God that is within you through the laying on of my hands [at his
> baptism], for God did not give us a spirit of cowardice but rather
> a spirit of power and of love and of self-discipline. (2 Tim 1:5-7)

In worship together, we believe for one another and with one another,
even when our own faith feels like a fire that has gone out, leaving
only cold ashes. On those days when we cannot pray ourselves, others
pray in our stead. When the song has gone from our lives, we sing for
one another.

Yes, we sing the affirmations of our faith too, perhaps in hymns
like "How Firm a Foundation" after the sermon. We sing these affirmations throughout worship with hymns that capture the meaning
of the faith through the centuries. We sing our faith, with the faith of
our minds descending to our hearts.

Old Testament theologian G. W. Anderson wrote an article he
titled "Israel's Creed: Sung, Not Signed."[7] He began with the Hebrew
creed, the *Shema*, which is sung in every Shabbat service. Faith is
better a song to be sung, he says, than a document to be signed. Likewise, the creeds are often more alive in song than they are on a page.

Religion scholar Marcus Borg was once asked after a lecture, "What do you think of the Apostles' Creed?" In answer, Borg spoke of the Creed's importance as a reservoir of the church's faith, then added that it is better sung than recited in worship. Bach's B-Minor Mass sings the Nicene Creed far more powerfully than words can speak it. Listening to it, the whole person is swept up in wonder and praise.

As I wrote in the "Prelude" to this book, growing up the son of a minister of music gave me a chance to sing the faith before I had to confess it. This sung faith was a "prevenient grace," preparing the ground for a faith that could grow without the constraints of literalism. So consider the value of a creed or affirmation of faith after the sermon or at other moments in worship. Worshipers need to affirm their faith together with the company of God's people.

Notes

1. Harvey Cox, *The Future of Faith* (New York: Harper One, 2009), 223.

2. Karen Armstrong, *The Case for God* (New York: Alfred A. Knopf, 2009), 87ff.

3. William Sloane Coffin, *Credo* (Louisville, KY: Westminster John Knox, 2004).

4. Rowan Williams, *Arius: Heresy and Tradition* (Grand Rapids, MI: Wm. B. Eerdmans, 2003), 24.

5. Christopher Morse, *Not Every Spirit: A Dogmatics of Christian Disbelief* (Harrisburg, PA: Trinity Press, 1994), 78.

6. *Book of Common Worship* (Louisville, KY: Westminster John Knox, 1993), 94-96.

7. G. W. Anderson, "Israel's Creed: Sung, Not Signed," *Scottish Journal of Theology* 16, no. 3 (1962): 16:21ff.

Chapter 8

The Prayers of the People

I need Thee every hour, most gracious Lord.[1]

In worship services, we set aside a holy moment for the prayers of the people of God, prayers of intercession and supplication. In some churches these prayers are offered after the sermon, and in others they come earlier in the service. Gail Ramshaw writes of intercessory prayer, "The words of prayer put God and the neighbor into our mouths and, it is hoped, into our hearts."[2]

Don Saliers says this form of prayer brings a central reality into focus: "Christ is in the midst of his people praying with them and for them." Our prayers show that we believe this. Saliers goes on to say that in intercessory prayer, there is vulnerability and empathy as we consider our relationships with others; there is solidarity with those for whom we pray; there is moral intentionality as we ask God to remember them and as we engage with the needs of others. Praying as a congregation can connect ministries of the church to those who need them. Intercessory prayer is strenuous, not passive.[3]

Some in the congregation have been waiting for this moment. Their prayers are wrung from their hearts. My present church is small enough to allow us to share our concerns publicly before we pray. This voicing of celebration and concern is always a poignant and powerful moment of our worship. We are vulnerable to one another and to God as in no other part of worship.

It is helpful to admit that we may bring doubts to intercessory prayer. In the middle of the intercessory prayer he was leading, a minister once exclaimed, "Lord, we bring these petitions every week!"

It was an honest cry, as honest as the psalms. Sometimes our doubts come by way of the bad theology about intercessory prayer we have heard through the years. Take, for example, the story of prayer told by Huckleberry Finn:

> Then Miss Watson she took me in the closet and prayed, but nothing come of it. She told me to pray every day, and whatever I asked for I would get it. But it warn't so. I tried it. Once I got a fishline, but no hooks. It warn't any good to me without hooks. I tried for hooks three or four times, but somehow I couldn't make it work. . . . I set down, one time back in the woods, and had a long think about it. I says to myself, if a body can get anything they pray for, why don't Deacon Winn get back the money he lost on pork? Why can't the widow get back her silver snuff-box that was stole? Why can't Miss Watson fat up? No, says I to myself, there ain't nothing in it.[4]

Huck Finn believed too little because Miss Watson believed too much. She turned prayer into magic. We are rightly put off by this kind of prayer. William James, whose masterpiece, *The Varieties of Religious Experience*, was the first great psychology of religion, described this kind of prayer as "lobbying in the courts of the Almighty for special favors."

We ought also to admit our intellectual stumbling blocks to intercessory prayer. Why would God spare some and not others; heal some and not others? Does God play favorites? How does prayer fit within our scientific worldview? Does God intervene in our history and our lives, and if so, how? In intercessory prayer, we may question our most fundamental concepts of God.

Then there are emotional stumbling blocks. We have all endured unanswered prayers. Our hearts, bruised with disappointment, may have made our prayers cautious. In fear of further disappointment, we may have even stopped praying such prayers. I know a woman whose best girlfriend died in high school. Watching her dear friend die caused her such trauma that the very mention of intercessory prayer brings her to anger.

But faith lives in the disappointment of unanswered prayer. The old hymn bravely sings, "Have faith in God when your prayers are unanswered."[5] Paul prayed fervently that God would remove his agonizing "thorn . . . in the flesh," but God did not free him of this affliction, whatever it was—physical, emotional, or psychological. Instead, God answered, "My grace is sufficient for you, for power is made perfect in weakness" (2 Cor 12:7, 9). Rather than healing grace, Paul was given sustaining grace, grace sufficient for the hour.

Religion scholar Obery Hendricks writes that Jesus's ministry demonstrated that our needs are holy to God. This is evidenced by how often Jesus prayed for the healing of others—healing of body, mind, and spirit. Following Jesus in intercessory prayer, in all its forms, is always an act of self-expanding love. It is no casual or cheap offering. Intercessory prayer is part of our calling as the people of God. In 1 Timothy, Paul writes, "First of all, then, I urge that supplications, prayers, intercessions, and thanksgivings be made for everyone." (2:1). The book of James instructs,

> Are any among you suffering? They should pray. Are any cheerful? They should sing songs of praise. Are any among you sick? They should call for the elders of the church and have them pray over them, anointing them with oil in the name of the Lord. (Jas 5:13-14)

There is no doubt that intercessory prayer has been a part of Christian worship from its beginnings.

In his helpful essay on intercessory prayer, Former Archbishop of Canterbury Rowan Williams says, "The prayer of intercession at its simplest is thinking of something or someone in the presence of God." He goes on to write of the struggle in it, its "agonistic" quality:

> *Then* it is a struggle alright, the struggle not to let God and the world fall apart from each other, because that is the centre of this prayer, the recognition that, in spite of appearances, God and the world belong together. It believes that intercessory prayer is at its basic the belief that God and the world belong together. . . . There is nowhere the love of God cannot go.[6]

It may be helpful to think of intercessory prayer as a sacred triangle made of the one praying, the one for whom we pray, and God. God with us.

Intercessory prayer is a school of compassion. In some Korean churches, the time of intercessory prayer has taken the form of what they call *Tongsung Kido*, or "prayed aloud." Everyone utters their prayers of supplication and intercession aloud simultaneously. What a beautiful cacophony of sound unto the Lord this must be!

I have been deeply moved by the ministry of intercessory prayer in the Iona Community off the west coast of Scotland. It takes a particular worship form every Tuesday evening in a Service of Intercessory Prayer. As you enter the Iona Abbey, you take your seat in the ancient Nave. When the first movement of worship is finished, all are invited to take part in the laying on of hands for healing, as receivers or givers of these prayers. In the opening between the Nave and the Choir, ten chairs are placed in a circle. Inside the circle are two or three members of the intercessory prayer ministry. Anyone wishing to receive the laying on of hands is invited to come sit in one of the ten chairs. One by one, each receives the laying on of hands, with the one laying on hands leading all who are present to pray these words for the person on whom their hands rest:

> Spirit of the Living God, present with us now,
> Enter your body, mind and spirit,
> and heal you of all that harms you.
> In Jesus' Name, Amen.[7]

After the first ten receive the prayers, others who have come forward take their places, and this continues until all who wish to receive prayer have done so. The others gathered for worship become part of these prayers in two ways. The first is by remaining in their seat and repeating the healing prayer over and over. The second is by going forward to the circle and placing their hands on the people seated in the circle or placing their hands on the shoulders of the person standing in front of them. The power of the sound of the prayer prayed aloud over and over is deeply touching. It pervades the air, cascading forth.

In my own ministry, I have adapted this prayer in two ways. The first has been to occasionally ask the congregation to say the Iona prayer together in morning worship at the time of intercessory prayers. They are invited to pray for someone in particular and, if comfortable, hold hands with the person beside them. And I have also led services of intercessory prayer, adapted from the Iona model, outside of the usual worship service.

Is there room for unspoken, unutterable prayers in worship? Yes—sometimes in the silences between the words, in the silence we may provide at the beginning of worship, or in the silence after the sermon or before or during the Prayers of the People. Often instrumental music can aide us in our silent prayer, as the Spirit intercedes with cries too deep for words. But praying aloud together unites us in ways that silent prayers cannot.

Notes

1. Robert Lowry (refrain) and Annie S. Hawks, "I Need Thee Every Hour," 1872, tune: NEED, https://hymnary.org/text/i_need_thee_every_hour_most_gracious_lor.

2. Gail Ramshaw, "Pried Open by Prayer," in Liturgy and the Moral Self (Collegeville, MN: Liturgical Press, 1998), 169.

3. Don E. Saliers, "Liturgy and Ethics: Some New Beginnings," in *Liturgy and the Moral Self* (Collegeville, MN: Liturgical Press, 1998), 28-30.

4. Mark Twain, *Huckleberry Finn* (1884; repr., Franklin Center, PA: The Franklin Library, 1979), 18.

5. B. B. McKinney, "Have Faith in God," 1934, tune: MUSKOGEE, https://hymnary.org/text/have_faith_in_god_when_your_pathway_is_l.

6. Rowan Williams, "Intercessory Prayer," in *Open to Judgement: Sermons and Addresses* (London: Darton, Longman & Todd, 1994), 138–39.

7. *The Iona Abbey Worship Book* (Glasgow: Wild Goose Publications, 2001), 91.

Chapter 9

The Offering of Oneself to God and to Christ's Service in the World

Praise God, from whom all blessings flow;
praise God, all creatures high and low:
Alleluia, alleluia!
Praise God in Jesus fully known;
Creator, Word, and Spirit one:
Alleluia, alleluia
alleluia, alleluia,
alleluia! [1]

After the prayers of the people comes the Offering—the offering of oneself to God and to Christ's service in the world. An instrumental Offertory is played, the collection plates are passed, and in some churches, those who have collected the offering come back down the aisle to the front. A minister might offer a prayer of dedication over the gifts. Something crucial has happened: the people of God have responded to all that has happened during this day of worship with the offering of themselves and their gifts to God. For me and many, this moment is the climax of worship.

In some of my churches, as the deacons came down the aisle from back to front with the gifts, the Doxology was played, the congregation singing, "Praise God from Whom All Blessings Flow." The worshipers stood as the gifts passed them, from the back row forward. By the time their offerings had reached the front, all were standing. The congregation seemed almost to have levitated. All those in the sanctuary had participated in the Offering, whether they placed anything in the collection plates or not. It was a eucharistic moment.

The first time I read Evelyn Underhill's classic on worship, I was alone in a cabin at night. She enumerated the four elements of true worship that I discussed in chapter 1. "Ritual," she listed first, and I said to myself, "Yes, Ritual." Then "Symbol." I said, "Yes, Symbol too." And "Sacraments," she wrote. Yes, I thought, "The Table, the Baptismal Pool, the Laying on of Hands." Then she named the fourth: "Sacrifice"! My reading slowed, and I put down my pen.

"Worship," Underhill wrote, is "summed up in sacrifice." When we meet the Divine, there is a sense of awe, but a sequel to this sense of awe is the feeling that we want, we need, to offer something to God. "Sacrifice" is "our first lesson in creaturely love." Sacrifice, she concludes, "unites the small movements of his [one's] childish soul to the eternal sacrifice of the Son."[2] The words of a well-loved Isaac Watts hymn come to mind:

> Were the whole realm of nature mine,
> that were a present far too small;
> love so amazing, so divine
> demands my life, my soul, my all.[3]

So does the Offering sum up our worship. We worship the one who emptied himself of divine glory for us and our salvation. We worship the one who "loving us loved us to the end" (see John 13:1), who spent his life for us every day of his ministry and poured it out fully on the cross for us.

The time of the Offering is difficult and sometimes painful for some in the pews. They may be in a tight financial time and cannot give as they would wish. Or they may have been in churches that made financial giving the proof of their devotion and faith. The "tithe" became law, a demand that some people, given their income, could not measure up to. In some churches, the Offering has become an exercise in church self-promotion or the pastor's self-promotion. And yet it is about far more than money. It is about God's self-expending love for us and for all people and about our own self-expending love for others. It is about all we offer to God every day.

The Offering is the time when we remember the woman who anointed Jesus with a rare perfume that cost a year's wages, and Jesus said of her extravagant act of devotion, "wherever this good news is proclaimed in the whole world, what she has done will be told in remembrance of her" (Matt 26:13). The Offering is the moment when we remember Jesus's commendation of the widow at the temple who gave "two small copper coins," not out of her excess of funds but from her daily needs (Luke 21:1-4). At the Offering, we remember the transformation of the rich tax collector Zacchaeus, who, changed by the Divine Friendship of Jesus, stood up in the middle of a meal and said, "Look, half of my possessions, Lord, I will give to the poor, and if I have defrauded anyone of anything, I will pay back four times as much" (Luke 19:8). And Jesus said, "Today, salvation has come to this house!" Social Gospel theologian Walter Rauschenbusch said of this astonishing moment: "Here a camel passed through the needle's eye and Jesus stood and cheered."[4] At the Offering, we remember Barnabas selling a piece of land and giving the proceeds to the church in Jerusalem, a great encouragement to that early, fledgling community (Acts 4:36-37).

At the Offering, we remember King David, singer of Israel and dancer before the Lord, who was "a man after [God's] own heart" (1 Sam 13:14; also see Acts 13:22). One day, he went to make a sacrifice to God at the threshing floor of a man named Araunah. He offered to buy the man's oxen, land, and wood for the sacrifice. When Araunah recognized he was David the king, he bowed and asked to give him the oxen, land, and wood. But David said, "No, but I will buy them from you for a price; I will not offer burnt offerings to the LORD my God that cost me nothing" (2 Sam 24:24; see also 1 Chr 21:24). On that spot and in that spirit, years later the temple in Jerusalem was built, a holy place where people would come near and far to worship the Lord and offer sacrifices.

Right in the middle of Paul's Second Letter to the Corinthians, he stops and urges an offering for the poor in Jerusalem, devoting two whole chapters to it. The climactic verse is "Each of you must give as you have made up your mind, not regretfully or under compulsion, for God loves a cheerful giver" (2 Cor 9:7). The Greek word for "cheerful" was *hilaron*, from which we get the word "hilarious." God loves hilarious givers, those who give freely and extravagantly out of love, the way lovers give to the one they love, sorry only that they do not have more to give.

In her book *Saints and Postmodernism: Revisioning Moral Philosophy*, Edith Wyschogrod writes that the saints shared this essence: they made a sumptuous sacrifice of self for the alleviation of the suffering of others and the birth of their joy. "Altruism in intrinsically excessive," she writes, and saints' own lives, their own bodies, become "sumptuaries" as they give of themselves in costly, extravagant ways.[5] We may not often give sumptuously, but when we do there is joy in it.

I have mentioned the Agape Meal at Broadway Baptist Church in Ft. Worth, Texas. As a center-city church, we had a seven-day-a-week ministry to the homeless and poor of the city through the Community Center. At the same time, we were in a two-million-dollar-plus fundraising campaign for building a new pipe organ to the glory of God, giving as the woman gave her extravagant gift of perfume to anoint Jesus's feet. At the end of one worship service, I went from my chair to the pulpit to announce our gifts to date. I had the total written on a piece of paper in my hand: $1,967,250.17. As I traveled to the pulpit, I asked myself, "Do I round off the figure?" I decided to read all the dollars and cents: "As of this Sunday, we have given one million, nine hundred and sixty-seven thousand, two hundred and fifty dollars and seventeen cents!"

A few minutes later, as I stood in the narthex after worship, a young boy came up to me from the side. He tugged on my robe. I bent down. He stood on tiptoes and whispered to me, "That was my seventeen cents!" I was so glad I had not rounded it off! God never rounds it off. Every seventeen-cent gift is important.

In today's world, many people give to church by check through the mail, by monthly bank draft, or online. Has the Offering then become a vestige of the past, a merely symbolic moment in worship? No, it is still crucial as a key movement of worship. It is about the whole giving of self to God. It is important for children to see adults give as an act of worship. In one church, we decided to give all the loose coins and bills taken in the offering each Sunday to our local mission for the poor and houseless. It was a little leap of faith; some feared it might impact our budget offerings. But it did not. The money given this way enlivened the Offering and was a boost to our mission. Everyone could give *something* at this moment in worship.

In my present church, the first Sunday of every month is Noisy Offering Sunday. The children come down the aisle with pots and pans, and we drop in our handfuls of loose change. That offering is given to houseless and poor families in the school district who need change for coin-operated laundries, a need we do not often think about. A joyful noise we make! And delight fills the room. In these ways and more, churches have reimagined and repeated that second-century worship service with offerings taken for the poor.

It is time now for the presentation of gifts and the Doxology. Praise be to God, source of all our gifts and blessings, for the gift of life itself in all its goodness.

I was worshiping in a Black church one Sunday. When the pastor announced that it was time for the offering, the congregation shouted aloud, "Thanks be to God!" That's the way to take an offering.

Notes

1. Brian A. Wren, "Praise God from Whom All Blessings Flow," tune: LASST UNS ERFREUEN (Hope Publishing Company, 1989).

2. Evelyn Underhill, *Worship* (London: Nisbet & Company, 1936), 47–48.

3. Isaac Watts, "When I Survey the Wondrous Cross," tune: HAMBURG, 1707, https://hymnary.org/text/when_i_survey_the_wondrous_cross_watts.

4. Walter Rauschenbusch, *The Social Principles of Jesus* (New York: Association Press, 1921), 68.

5. Edith Wyschogrod, *Saints and Postmodernism: Revisioning Moral Philosophy* (Chicago: University of Chicago Press, 1990), 146–47.

Chapter 10

The Service of the Table—Meanings and Practice

"He is turning water into wine. . . . He is expecting new guests, He is calling new ones unceasingly forever and ever." (Dostoevsky, *The Brothers Karamazov*)[1]

No moment in worship is more like a holy ballet than Communion. The priests make their way to the altar, the minister breaks the bread and pours the cup, the people come to the altar and kneel to receive the bread and cup, or the deacons fan out into the aisles to distribute the elements and the people pass the bread and cup to each other as the music plays—it feels like sacred dance.

The past, present, and future, all the world, the Communion of Saints, and all those present are gathered to one great feast. In Dostoyevsky's masterpiece of a novel, *The Brothers Karamazov*, Father Zossima, an old priest drenched in holiness who has lived in the incredible joy of the kingdom, dies. His body lies in a coffin in a monastery where a priest reads John 2:1-11 about Jesus turning water into wine at the wedding feast at Cana. Alyosha, a young man who loved Father Zossima, comes into the room. As he kneels to pray and hears the priest reading the text, he falls asleep and begins to dream about the wedding feast. The room where the feast is happening begins to grow wider and wider until Alyosha himself is there. Then an old man from the table rises and comes toward him.

It is Father Zossima, who says, "Why have you hidden yourself here, out of sight? We are drinking the new wine, the wine of new and great joy!" And then he calls to Alyosha, telling him to look at Jesus who is there, and he tells him, "He is changing the water into wine. . . . He is expecting new guests, He is calling new ones unceasingly forever and ever."[2]

This is the joy and wonder of the Eucharist!

Gregory Dix, in his comprehensive work *The Shape of the Liturgy*, calls the Eucharist "the representative act of a fully redeemed person." This person is not the "Acquisitive Man," always dissatisfied and wanting more, or the "Mass-Man," the dehumanized person living as a cog in an economic industrial wheel, but rather the "Eucharistic Man" giving thanks to God and taking part of a worshiping community grounded in eternity.[3]

Variously called the Lord's Supper, Communion, Holy Communion, and the Eucharist, the Service of the Table has through the years been composed of these parts in one form or another:

The Prayer of Thanksgiving
The Words of Institution
The Prayer of Consecration, or Epiclesis
The Distribution of the Bread and Cup
A Concluding Prayer of Thanksgiving
The Sharing of the Peace

Of the principal meanings of the Meal, we begin with Thanksgiving. In the New Testament Greek, the word "Eucharist" means gift, grace, or gratitude. Above all we are here to receive the grace of God and give thanks to God for God's good gifts. James McClendon writes that the meal is "inseparable from awed gratitude."[4] James White notes that in Calvin's Eucharistic rite, thanksgiving is almost submerged in its "moral earnestness."[5]In many churches the invitation to the table emphasizes the moral conditions to receive the sacrament, and the tone of thanksgiving—grace, gift, and awed gratitude—is diminished.

The Service of the Table partakes of the four actions of Jesus at the table of the Last Supper but also at other occasions, including the feeding of the multitudes and the meal he ate with the disciples at

Emmaus as the Risen Lord. He *took* the bread and *blessed* it, *broke* it, and *gave* it. This taking, blessing, breaking, and giving are the heart of the Eucharist.

As Gregory Dix traces the historical "shape of the liturgy" in the Eucharist, he discusses how the classic shape of the Eucharist has remained remarkably unchanged since the first three centuries. He concludes that at its essential core, it is the action (doing) of the whole Body of Christ at worship, not something done for them. He uses the liturgical term "Synaxis," which means "meeting," to describe the worship service that leads up to the Eucharist—the opening words, song, texts, and sermon.

Then Dix describes the four-fold actions of the Eucharist that follow from Jesus's four-fold actions at the table.[6] The first is the "Invocation" where the bread and cup are brought to the Table. In churches where the Offering follows the Sermon and Prayers, the bringing of the bread and cup proceeds from the bringing of the Offering to God. It makes perfect spiritual sense as the "Synaxis" portion of the worship service now leads to Communion.

The second element is the "Eucharistic Prayer" or "Great Prayer of Thanksgiving" over the bread and cup (early called the "cup of blessing" from its Jewish roots), which will be discussed below. The earliest use and form we know comes from Hippolytus in his *Apostolic Traditions*.

The third element is the "Fraction," or the breaking of the bread.

And the fourth is the "Communion," where both bread and wine are distributed. Together, these elements are the Eucharist, or Thanksgiving to God, and the receiving of the gifts of God at the table of grace.

After the first meaning of the Table as Eucharist, its second meaning is Commemoration, a remembering that re-members us to the saving work of God in history and through Christ. The word often used here is *anamnesis*, which is more than a remembering of the past; the past is brought into the present. The past is present now. "Do this in remembrance of me," Jesus said at the Last Supper (Luke 22:19). We remember his giving of himself at the cross for us and for the salvation of the many. But there is more that we remember, and we will discuss this when we address the Great Prayer of Thanksgiving.

A third meaning of the Table is Forgiveness. As Jesus said that night at the table, "this is my blood of the covenant, which is poured out for many for the forgiveness of sins" (Matt 26:28). Forgiveness can happen here. As a young theological student in New York City, I went to St. John Cathedral and participated for the first time in an Anglican Eucharist. As I came to the front in that cavernous space—its nave the largest in the world—and knelt to receive Communion, the priest placed the bread and cup to my mouth and said the words, I suppose something like "the Body of Christ, the Blood of Christ." But what I heard and felt was "Your sins are forgiven." *Are forgiven*! There is pardon here but also power, the grace of new life.

Fourth, the Table means Communion, that is, the experience of *koinonia*, the fellowship of the Holy Spirit as we gather around that sacred Table. The Anabaptists emphasized this dimension in their theology of the church.

A fifth dimension is the Work of the Holy Spirit. We pray an *epiclesis*, a prayer of consecration, asking the Spirit to bring the presence of Christ to us in the bread and wine and transform them into something more—a prayer for God's feeding of us in them. "Bread of heaven, Bread of heaven, feed me till I want no more." [7]

A sixth dimension of the Table is eschatological: the Meal of the Kingdom of God. It is a foretaste of the festive meal of God's kingdom in the world to come. Jesus pointed us to this idea in his words at the Last Supper in Luke:

> "I have eagerly desired to eat this Passover with you before I suffer, for I tell you, I will not eat it until it is fulfilled in the kingdom of God." Then, he took a cup, and after giving thanks he said, "Take this and divide it among yourselves, for I tell you that from now on I will not drink of the fruit of the vine until the kingdom of God comes." (Luke 22:15-18)

It is more than a foretaste: as we partake of the bread and wine, we are eating and feasting with Jesus now. We are experiencing the words of Jesus: "people will come from east and west, from north and south, and take their places at the banquet in the kingdom of God" (Luke 13:29). It is happening now, and the Table stretches all over the globe.

Charles and John Wesley wrote more than one hundred Eucharistic hymns that set to song and lyrics all the meanings of the Eucharist. The hymn "Come, Let Us Join with One Accord" expresses the eschatological meaning of the Eucharist:

> By faith and hope already here
> Ev'n now the marriage-feast we share,
> Ev'n now we by the Lamb are fed,
> Our Lord's celestial joy we prove.[8]

At the Table, the "then" of the great feast of the kingdom of God is now.

Now we turn to the practice of the Eucharist. Each meaning of the Eucharist is enacted in the Service of the Table, and the Eucharistic Prayer (or Prayer of Thanksgiving or Great Prayer of Thanksgiving) speaks of them all. James McClendon asks, "Can the meal become a story?" Yes, and the Prayer of Thanksgiving begins the story of the Long Mercy of God in Creation and Redemption and on to Consummation. At the Table we recite the "mystery of our faith": "Christ has died, Christ is risen, Christ shall come again." It is all there, interspersed with music—like the Sanctus, which unites the "Holy, Holy, Holy" of the seraphim in Isaiah's vision to Matthew's account of Jesus's triumphal entry into Jerusalem. It's all there: the great story of God with us and for us for all time!

Here is the "Great Thanksgiving" and Eucharistic Liturgy from *The United Methodist Book of Worship*:

> The Lord be with you.
> And also with you.
> Lift up your hearts
> We lift them up to the Lord
> Let us give thanks and praise.
> It is right to give our thanks and praise.

It is right, and a good and joyful thing,
always and everywhere, to give thanks to you,
Father Almighty, creator of heaven and earth.

You formed us in your image
and breathed into us the breath of life.
When we turned away, and our love failed,
your love remained steadfast.
You delivered us from captivity,
made covenant to be our sovereign God,
and spoke to us in the prophets.

And so,

with your people on earth
and all the company of heaven
we praise your name and join their unending song:

Holy, holy, holy Lord, Lord of power and might,
heaven and earth are full of your glory.
Hosanna in the highest,
Blessed is he who comes in the name of the Lord.
Hosanna in the highest!

And now, moving to the story of Jesus:

Holy are you, and blessed is your Son Jesus Christ.
Your Spirit anointed him
to preach good news to the poor,
to proclaim release to captives
and recovering of sight to the blind,
to set at liberty those who were oppressed,
and to announce that the time had come
when you would save your people.
He healed the sick, fed the hungry, and ate with sinners.
By the baptism of his suffering, death and resurrection
you gave birth to your Church,
delivered us from slavery to sin and death,

and made with us a new covenant
by water and the Spirit.
When the Lord ascended,
he promised to be with us always,
in the power of your Word and Holy Spirit.

Then, from the same *Book of Worship*, the words of Institution. The presider takes the bread and lifts it and says,

On the night in which he gave himself up for us,
he took the bread, gave thanks to you, broke the bread,
gave it to his disciples, and said,
"Take, eat, this is my body, which is given for you.
Do this in remembrance of me."

The presider lifts and or pours the cup and says,

When the supper was over, he took the cup,
gave thanks to you, gave it to the disciples, and said
"Drink from this, all of you;
this is the blood of the new covenant,
poured out for you and for many
for the forgiveness of sins.
Do this, as often as you drink it, in remembrance of me."

And so,

In remembrance of these, your mighty acts in Jesus Christ,
we offer ourselves in praise and thanksgiving
as a holy and living sacrifice,
in union with Christ's offering for us,
as we proclaim the mystery of faith.
Christ has died; Christ has risen; Christ will come again.

Now the Prayer for the Holy Spirit, or Epiclesis:

Pour out your Holy Spirit upon us gathered here,
and in these gifts of bread and wine.

Make them be for us the body and blood of Christ,
that we might be for the world the body of Christ,
redeemed in his blood.
By your Spirit, make us one with Christ,
one with each other,
and one in ministry to all the world,
until we feast at his heavenly banquet.

Through your Son Jesus Christ,
with the Holy Spirit in your holy Church,
all honor and glory is yours, almighty Father,
now and forever. Amen.

Then follows the Lord's Prayer, the Breaking of the Bread, and the
Giving of the Bread and Cup. There is an exchange of words as the
elements are given and received:

The Body of Christ, given for you.
Amen
The blood of Christ given for you.
Amen.

Then comes the Final Prayer of Thanksgiving:

Eternal God, we give you thanks for this holy mystery
in which you have given yourself to us.
Grant that we may go forth into the world
in the strength of your Spirit,
to give ourselves for others,
in the name of Jesus Christ our Lord. Amen.[9]

Last is the Sharing of the Peace.

The Sharing of the Peace of Christ is often practiced as the final
act of the Service of the Table. While some churches place it early
in the service, for me it has special power and significance after the
giving and receiving of the bread and cup. As Paul wrote, "For he
(Christ) is our peace; in his flesh he has made both into one [Jew and
Gentile] and has broken down the dividing wall, that is, the hostility

between us" (Eph 2:14) Every wall between us and God and between us and others has come down. This oneness is made startlingly clear in a revolutionary way in Paul's words to the Galatians:

> As many of you as were baptized into Christ have clothed your-selves with Christ. There is no longer Jew or Greek; there is no longer slave or free; there is no longer male and female, for all of you are one in Christ Jesus. (Gal 3:27-28)

Early Baptists were not timid about calling Communion and Baptism "sacraments," acknowledging them to be "means of grace." Later they preferred to call these sacred actions "ordinances," that is, followed in obedience to Christ's commands. But perhaps we in the Free Church tradition should consider the Baptismal Pool and the Communion Table sacramental. To recognize them as sacraments is to realize that God is acting among us. The Table is a "meeting place" with God, who has promised to meet us there. It is a "rendezvous with God, a trysting place." The Celtic Christians called such places "thin places," places and moments where the veil between earth and heaven becomes so thin that we experience earth and heaven as one.

Because many Baptists have reduced the meaning of the Table to an ordinance, what was once called "sacrament" becomes "mere symbol" or "mere memorial." But can any sacred act in worship be called "mere"? Reducing the Eucharist to mere anything has led to it being practiced sporadically or infrequently in worship: once a quarter, once a month, once a year. Personally, I love this sacrament and would gladly have the Service of the Table in every Sunday's worship, especially in Advent and Lent, and yet every church must determine the frequency that gives the Eucharist the most meaning for them. Most of the churches I have served have elected to cele-brate Communion once a month on Sunday mornings and then at important days and festivals of the Christian year: for example, Christmas Eve, Ash Wednesday, Maundy Thursday, Pentecost, and World Communion Sunday.

The Eucharistic Service of the United Methodists detailed earlier in this chapter may be too liturgically formal for many churches, but major parts of it can be improvised to take on the vernacular of the people. The minister thus gives thanks, as Justin Martyr says in his description of worship, "according to his ability." Hippolytus, even as he set out the historic form, allowed for the freedom of those presiding at the meal.

In conclusion, I offer two more meanings of the Eucharist, the Eucharist as Healing and the Eucharist as Conversion. It is the testimony of many that the receiving of the bread and wine was a healing event. In the words of the Roman Mass, the invitation to the Table is an invitation to healing, echoing the healing story of the servant in Matthew 8:5-13:

> Lord, I am not worthy
> to have you come under my roof;
> but only speak the word
> and my soul will be healed. (See Luke 7:7)

I once spent a month at St. John's Abbey, where the Eucharist is offered every day. I came to the Table daily, with the Benedictine's blessing, and with these words of invitation in my ear, I felt soul healing happening.

John Wesley served the Eucharist in the streets to the unbaptized because he believed it to be a "converting sacrament." I'm convinced this happens in the lives of those who have come to faith by the taking of Communion. My earliest memory of church was sneaking back into the building on Communion Sundays when I was around four or five years old and drinking the leftover grape juice from the tiny glass cups. Who knows—maybe by God's prevenient grace, something was happening in that "untransubstantiated" Welch's.

Simone Weil, one of the twentieth century's great spiritual writers, grew up in an agnostic Jewish home. Even as a young girl, she possessed a tender conscience, especially toward the suffering, and became a teacher and part of the Socialist Workers Movement. Falling ill, she came to a monastery in Spain to convalesce. There she met an English priest who introduced her to the mystical poetry of George Herbert. She read his poems when she suffered migraine headaches and found that they eased her pain. One day as she read aloud Herbert's poem "Love Bade Me Welcome," her recitation of the poem took on, in her words "the virtue of a prayer," and "Christ himself came down and took possession of me."[10]Here is the poem:

Love bade me welcome: yet my soul drew back,
Guilty of dust and sin.
But quick-ey'd Love, observing me grow slack
From my first entrance in,
Drew nearer to me, sweetly questioning,
If I lack'd anything.

A guest, I answer'd, worthy to be here:
Love said, You shall be he.
I the unkind, ungrateful? Ah my dear,
I cannot look on thee.
Love took my hand, and smiling did reply,
Who made the eyes but I?

Truth Lord, but I have marr'd them: let my shame
Go where it doth deserve.
And know you not, says Love, who bore the blame?
My dear, then I will serve.
You must sit down, says Love, and taste my meat:
So I did sit and eat.[11]

It is indeed Love that brings us to the Table.

Notes

1. Fyodor Dostoevsky, *The Brothers Karamazov* (New York: Heritage, 1949), 277.

2. Dostoevsky, *The Brothers Karamazov.*

3. Gregory Dix, *The Shape of the Liturgy* (Westminster: Dacre Press, 1949), xviii.

4. James Wm. McClendon, *Systematic Theology*, vol. 2, *Doctrine*(Nashville: Abingdon Press, 1994), 405.

5. James White, *The Sacraments in Protestant Faith and Practice* (Nashville, Tennessee: Abingdon Press, 1999), 101.

6. Dix, *Shape of the Liturgy*, 48.

7. "Guide Me, O Thou Great Jehovah," in *The Worshipping Church: A Hymnal* (Carol Stream, IL: Hope Publishing Company, 1990), no. 634.

8. Charles Wesley, "Come, Let Us Join with One Accord, tune: BEATITUDO. 1763, https://hymnary.org/text/come_let_us_join_with_one_accord_in_hymn.

9. *United Methodist Book of Worship*, 36–39.

10. Simone Weil, *The Simone Weil Reader*, ed. George A. Panichas (New York: D. McKay, 1977), 16.

11. George Herbert, "Love (III)," in *George Herbert: The Country Parson and The Temple* (New York: Paulist Press, 1981), 316. Ralph Vaughn Williams has set this poem in an extraordinary way to music in his Five Mystical Songs.

Chapter 11

The Sending Forth, Benediction, and Blessing

Into the liturgy the people bring their entire existence so that it may be gathered up in praise. From the liturgy the people depart with a renewed vision of the value-patterns of God's kingdom, by the more effective practice of which they intend to glorify God in their whole life.[1]

It is time for the people of God to be sent forth into the world in two final acts of worship. The first is a sending forth into the world to do the work of the gospel, and the second is the blessing of God upon us as we leave, an act so vital that it has been passed down to us from Aaron's own blessing, given at the end of the earliest Hebrew worship (see Num 6:22-27).

A priest says at the end of worship, "Mass is ended. Go now to love and serve the Lord." Recalling Frederick Buechner's description, to this point in worship, we have done the things we need to do, the prayers and hymns and service of the Word and Table. Now we are about to depart to do the things God needs done: "run errands for him, carry messages for him, fight on his side, feed his lambs."[2]

Some traditions have a spoken "Charge" as the sending forth. The Presbyterian *Book of Common Worship* provides many examples, like this one:

Go out into the world in peace.
Love the Lord your God
with all your heart,

with all your soul,
with all your mind;
and love your neighbor as yourself.[3]

The Charge is best when short. It may quote biblical language, as in this example based on Micah 6:8: "God has shown you what is good. What does the Lord require of you but to do justice and to love mercy and to walk humbly with your God?" At Grace Baptist Church at the end of every monthly Communion service, we form a circle and sing a beautiful round version of this verse from Micah.[4] It voices the heart of the congregation's mission in the world. Additionally, this charge widely used by Henri-Frédéric Amiel is a beautiful example of one that does not use Scripture:

"Life is short,
An we don't have much time
  to gladden the hearts of those who make the journey with us.
So be swift to love,
  and make haste to be kind.[5]

The Charge should not be a recap of the sermon by a minister who wants one more crack at delivering the message. Someone said that good communication means, "Say what you are going to say; say it; then tell them what you have just said." That definition breaks a key rule of communication: respect your audience!

The Charge should be the penultimate words of the service, not the final ones. The last sacred words of worship are the words of Blessing and Benediction. Worship began with a greeting that was an exchange of blessing. Now at the end is the bestowal of blessing by the minister or priest.

Old Testament theologian Claus Westermann writes that God's salvation comes in two forms, salvation as deliverance and salvation as blessing. We often ignore the meaning of salvation as blessing, healing, wholeness, the daily ways God provides and cares for us. Worship, Westermann writes, should provide a place for both kinds of salvation.[6] We have talked about how important it is in worship to remember and recount God's acts of deliverance. Now it is time to receive the blessing of God as the healing, saving act it is. This last act of worship, Benediction and Blessing, is more important than we sometimes grasp. One of the most essential needs of every person is to be and feel blessed. People need to leave worship with blessings ringing in their ears and hearts.

Paul often ends his letters with a blessing. He sends blessing to the Philippians: "The grace of the Lord Jesus Christ be with your spirit" (Phil 4:23). And in his second letter to the Corinthians, he closes, "The grace of the Lord Jesus Christ, the love of God, and the communion of the Holy Spirit be with all of you" (2 Cor 13:13). Paul's words are often used in some form as the benediction at the end of worship. We may at no other moment of our week feel blessed, so it is a holy act to end worship with blessing and benediction.

From ancient times, people have hungered to leave worship with a blessing, with the assurance that the One they have come to worship will now go with them. For this reason God gave to Aaron, the first priest of Israel, and to all the ones who would follow in his lineage the immortal words they were to say as the people left worship:

The LORD bless and keep you;
the LORD make his face to shine upon you
and be gracious to you;
the LORD lift up his countenance upon you
and give you peace. (Num 6:24-26)

Let us examine each phrase.

"Bless and keep you." God's blessing is given and will now follow us. As the promise that ends the 23rd Psalm assures us: "Surely goodness and mercy shall follow me all the days of my life" (v. 6).

"Make his face to shine upon you and be gracious to you." How wonderful to see the face of someone we love light up and shine with joy to see our own face. We need in our mind's eye to see God's face shining on us, God's delight in us as God looks at us. It is an experience of grace.

"Lift up his countenance upon you." Here is God's face, not turned away in anger or down in disappointment but lifted to catch our eyes, which are now lifted to see God's face. Psychologists tell us of the crucial bond of mother and child as they see each other and mirror delight. This is primal grace.

"And give you peace." This peace is *shalom*, well-being within yourself and with others and with life itself. It is the shalom of Julian of Norwich's vision of what is to come: "All shall be well, and all shall be well, and all manner of thing shall be well." If our worship began with the greeting, "Grace and peace to you from the Lord Jesus Christ," so it now ends with the bestowal of grace and peace.

My sense of the power of the Benediction was given to me while I was pastor of Crescent Hill Baptist Church. One of my predecessors there, who left an indelible mark on the church, was John Claypool, a premier preacher of his day. I had long admired his preaching, but at Crescent Hill I discovered how important and beloved was the benediction he gave as he walked down the aisle at the end of the service:

> Depart now in the fellowship of God,
> and as you go, remember:
> By the goodness of God you were brought into this world;
> By the grace of God you have been kept all the day long,
> even unto this hour;
> And by the love of God, fully revealed in the face of Jesus,
> You are being redeemed.

It was a transformative benediction. It was healing for people brought up in an Original Sin tradition to hear that we were born in the goodness of God. We experienced the Original Blessing of God in that moment. To be reminded that grace had sustained our lives and brought us to worship that morning was a powerful recognition that life is a gift, to use Claypool's words, every hour and every day of it. And the final words: "You are being redeemed." God is not through with us yet! God is at work in us now. Salvation is a daily process, a journey we are on together toward redemption.

While I served at Crescent Hill, Claypool came back to preach for us on an important church anniversary. I discovered that the church not only longed to hear him preach again but also (perhaps even more) longed to hear him say his benediction again. A chord was struck in me.

Not long after, I read a benediction by William Sloane Coffin, given, as I remember, at a school convocation. I adapted it slightly and began to use it (with his permission) at the end of every service at Crescent Hill and in the churches I have served since:

> May the Lord bless and keep you.
> May the Lord make his Face to shine upon you
> And be gracious to you.
>
> May God give you the grace never to sell yourself short,
> The grace to risk something big for something good,
> The grace to remember
> That the world is too dangerous for anything but truth
> And too small for anything but love.
>
> So, may God take your minds and think through them,
> May God take your lips and speak through them,
> May God take your hearts
> And set them on fire!
> In Jesus's Name, Amen.

The first stanza comes from Aaron's benediction in Numbers 26. The second stanza is the pure brilliance of William Sloane Coffin:

"May God give you the grace never to sell yourself short." Heads pop up among people hearing this for the first time. It is unexpected, but that is the purpose of benediction. It lifts us from the dreary messages that say, "Don't think too much of yourself. Be humble. Play small. You'll never amount to anything," and on and on. This is benediction as an invigorating call to be what God has created and called us to be.

"Grace to risk something big for something good." We live such timid lives, refusing to take risks for what is truly good, afraid of failing or being seen as fools or, on the other hand, of taking big risks for things not so good. But we are called to a life of courage and boldness for the sake of God and God's kingdom.

"Grace to remember that the world is too dangerous for anything but truth." The world may have always been dangerous, but it seems more dangerous today, and truth is the first defense against its dangers.

"And too small for anything but love." The well-known photograph of Earth taken by the *Apollo* astronauts from the moon showed us the planet as one beautiful, jewel-like globe. Whether we recognize it or not, we are one. We belong to one another. Only love will save us.

And in the last stanza, the first phrase is attributed to W. H. Aitken, Canon of Norwich Cathedral (1841–1927):

> May God take your minds and think through them,
> May God take your lips and speak through them,
> May God take your hearts [and here comes the final surprise]
> And set them on fire!

We might expect something more conventional, like "take our hearts and fill them with love." But this benediction asks for "fire"—the fire of love, the fire of truth, the fire of justice, the fire of holiness!

When Blaise Pascal, the seventeenth century mathematician, scientist, and spiritual writer, died, a piece of parchment was found sewn into the lining of his clothes:

> The year of Grace 1654 . . .
> FIRE.
> God of Abraham, God of Isaac, God of Jacob,
> not the philosophers and scholars.
> Certainty, certainty, heart felt, joy and peace.
> God of Jesus Christ,
> My God and your God.
> Joy, joy, tears of joy . . .[7]

Indeed, FIRE.

This story is told from the Early Desert Fathers:

Abba Lot went to Abba Joseph and said to him, "Abba, as far as I can, I say my little office, fast a little, I pray and meditate, I live in peace and as far as I can, purify my thoughts. What else can I do?" Then the old man stood up and stretched out his hands towards heaven. His fingers became like ten lamps of fire, and he said to him, "If you will, you can become all flame."[8]

That is the way to leave worship!

A few decades ago, an amulet, a small piece of silver to be worn around the neck, was discovered in an archeological dig in Israel. It was found in an excavated house, and inscribed on it was the oldest example of Hebrew writing yet found. Dating around the fifth or sixth century BCE, these hallowed words were inscribed on it to be cherished forever: "The Lord bless you and keep you"—the first benediction of Hebrew worship, and ours even today.

We need to leave worship with God's blessing upon us—and God's fire within us!

Notes

1. Geoffrey Wainwright, *Doxology: The Praise of God in Worship, Doctrine, and Life (A Systematic Theology)* (New York: Oxford University Press, 1980), 8.

2. Frederick Buechner, *Wishful Thinking: A Theological ABC* (New York: Harper & Row, 1973), 97–98.

3. *Book of Common Worship*, 159.

4. *The Faith We Sing* (Nashville: Abingdon Press: 2000), #2174.

5. Henri-Frédéric Amiel, "16 Dec 1868," in *Amiel's Journal: The Journal Intime*, vol. 2, trans. Mrs. Humphrey Ward, (n.p.: Macmillan, 1899), 15.

6. Claus Westermann, *Blessing in the Bible and in the Life of the Church* (Philadelphia: Fortress Press, 1968), 111.

7. Blaise Pascal, "Memorial," quoted in Malcolm Muggeridge, "Pascal," in *The Third Testament* (Boston: Little, Brown and Company, 1976), 66.

8. "Joseph of Panephysis," in *The Sayings of the Desert Fathers: The Alphabetical Collection*, vol. 59, trans. Benedicta Ward (London and Oxford: Mowbray, 1981), 103.

Part 3

The Calling of Music in the Worship of God

"A gospel shout
And a gospel song:
Life is short
But God is long."[1]

Note

1. Langston Hughes, "Tambourines," in *Selected Poems of Langston Hughes* (New York: Random House, Vintage Classics, 1990), 29.

Chapter 12

The Calling of Sacred Music

Each time we experience a sacred call, we are instantly drawn into our true nature . . . which Joseph Campbell describes as "That interior, ineffable source of being, consciousness and bliss."[1]

For those who plan and lead church music, the task is more than a job or profession. It is a calling, a vocation. Frederick Buechner writes of vocation, "The kind of work God usually calls you to is the kind of work (a) that you most need to do and (b) that the world needs to have done."[2] It is the meeting place, as he says, between our deep gladness and the world's great need. It thus connects us with our deepest self. As David Cooper wrote, "Each time we experience a sacred call, we are instantly drawn into our true nature."[3] Such is the calling of sacred music that God gives to the people of God for the worship of God.

There are many callings in the body of the church to Christ's service of love in the world. Baptism is the ordination of all believers to be ministers: a Sunday school teacher of children, a person baking the Communion bread, a public schoolteacher giving their best to their students, a person doing the little and unheralded things that make life better for others. All of these represent the calling of love. Martin Luther challenged the Roman Catholic view that said the religious vocation to serve the church was the only true vocation. He famously insisted that the cobbler making shoes had as much of a calling as a monk saying his prayers. This chapter is about the unique calling of sacred music.

Music is a sacrament of God and therefore a sacrament of grace. Sacred music is a gift prompted by God's Spirit that calls us by its beautiful voice to return to God, our origin and destiny, and to bring our full selves before God's Presence. To use Paul's terms, it is a *charism*, or *charismata*, a gift of the Spirit. But sacred music is also a *spiritual practice* that demands an almost monk-like devotion from the leader of sacred music to learn skills that perfect the gift.

People speak about styles, or genres, of sacred music. Insisting on these divisions can cause counter-spiritual contentiousness. We can succumb to the human mania to be "separate and superior," to use Richard Rohr's incisive phrase.[4] Here is the crux of the matter: does the music, of whatever style, help us return to God and bring our full selves before God? Does it, following the movement of worship outlined in part 2, help us bring our praise, thanksgiving, awe, and delight? Does it help us bring the deepest confessions of the undefended self? Does it help us bring our sadness and our laments to God? Does it deepen our love of God and our devotion to God?

In his essay "On Church Music," C. S. Lewis writes of the kind of church music and church musician that serves or hinders our movement toward God. He writes from the Anglican worship tradition, as we can see from his own predilections, but his words offer profound guidance to all ministers and church musicians. I quote at length for its full impact:

> There are two musical situations on which I think we can be confident that a blessing rests.
>
> One is where a priest or an organist, himself a man of trained and delicate taste, humbly and charitably sacrifices his own (aesthetically right) desires and gives the people humbler and coarser fare than he would wish (even, as it may be, the erroneous belief) that he can thus bring them to God. The other is where the stupid and unmusical layman humbly and patiently, and above all silently, listens to music which he cannot, or cannot fully, appreciate, in the belief that it somehow glorifies God, and that if it does not edify him, this must be his own defect. Neither such a High Brow nor such a Low Brow can be far out the way. To both, Church Music will have been a means of grace, not the music

they have liked, but the music they have disliked. They have both offered and sacrificed their taste in the fullest sense.

But where the opposite situation arises, where the musician is filled with the pride of skill or the virus of emulation and looks with contempt on the unappreciative congregation, or where the unmusical, complacently entrenched in their own ignorance and conservatism, looks with the restless and resentful hostility of an inferiority complex on all who would try to improve their taste—there, we may be sure, all that both offer is unblessed and that the spirit that moves them is not of the Holy Ghost.

But Lewis concludes, "Where both the choir and the congregation are spiritually on the right road, no insurmountable difficulties will occur. Discrepancies of taste and capacity will, indeed, provide matter for mutual charity and humility."[5] These words have guided me more than a few times through the years.

The calling of church music, as for all vocations, is composed of three dimensions. The first is pleasure. If church musicians feel pleasure in the preparation and offering of music, congregations will experience pleasure as well. Worship pleasing to God evokes God's good pleasure (*eudokia*) in us and our pleasure in God. Wendell Berry writes of pleasure and work and says that pleasure is "both an empowerment of work and its indispensable measure."[6]

A second dimension is hard work. The church musician has undergone years of work and training to be able to present their skills as an offering to God and the people of God. It is hard, sometimes lonely work. Some days they would rather be doing something else and be somewhere other than the practice room!

In Pablo Casals's autobiography *Joys and Sorrows*, he tells of going mountain climbing near San Francisco. A boulder above him broke loose and hurtled toward him. It smashed his left hand, his fingering hand for the cello. His friends nearby were horrified, but Casals had this response: ". . . when I looked at my mangled bloody fingers, I had a strangely different reaction. My first thought was, 'Thank God I'll never have to play the cello again.'"[7] His hand, thank you, God, was restored, but his reaction gives us something honest to ponder. Any gift from God carries heavy responsibility that we would rather pass up some days. For Casals, at the time the world's most famous cellist and perhaps the world's most famous musician, his dedication to his gifts involved, in his words, "a sort of enslavement," and there was often for him, again in his own words, "a dreadful anxiety" before a performance.

We are all tempted to give up on the best gifts we can offer the world because of what they demand of us. Some days despair hits, other days a fear of failure, and on other days we are just bone tired. But we should not give up. We are what we alone can best offer the world. To give that up would be to lose part of our truest and deepest selves.

A third dimension of calling involves integrity. Casals offers us another personal story: He was hurrying from the train to Paris to perform the Dvořák *Cello Concerto* and went directly to the music hall for the rehearsal. Shortly before the rehearsal, the conductor, Gabriel Pierné, showed up in Casals's dressing room to discuss the score. At some point Pierné tossed the music aside and said, "What a ghastly piece of music!"

Casals at first thought he was joking, but Pierné went on to say, "It's hardly worth playing. It's not really music at all." Casals stared at him uncomprehendingly, then said, "How can you talk that way about such a magnificent work?" If that's the way you feel about the work, he continued, "then you're clearly not capable of conducting it. Since I happen to love the music, I couldn't take part in its desecration. And I won't. I refuse to play." And he did. The conductor had to go on stage and announce Casals's refusal to play. Later, Casals was fined 3,000 francs, no small sum. But Casals said later, "I would act the same way today. Either you believe in what you are doing or you do not. Music is something to be approached with integrity, not something to be turned on and off like tap water."[8]

So too is the integrity of the church musician at work. Such integrity entails three parts. The first part is to serve the manuscript of music as best you can. You learn not only the notes but also the composer's intention without imposing your will upon it.

Second, integrity means to serve God as best you can. As Bach inscribed all his manuscripts SDG, *Soli Deo Gloria*, to the Glory of

God Alone, so we inscribe our work "as unto the Lord," to use Paul's phrasing. This form of integrity is a form of kneeling before God, offering what you offer as a sacrifice of praise.

The third part of integrity for the church musician is serving the people of God. We help them bring their real selves before God. Sacred music is not a vain exercise to raise a congregation's musical literacy but rather a vehicle to help them love God with all their hearts, minds, souls, and might.

One more story from Casals addresses this role of music as a servant. When he was a young boy, Casals took piano lessons and studied piano improvisation. When he overindulged himself in some intricate harmony, his teacher wrapped his arms around the boy's shoulders and said, "Pablito, in the language of everybody—Yes?"[9]

We serve God best as we use the musical "language of everybody." Such music imitates God, who in the Incarnation of Jesus spoke to us in the language of everybody. As I have sought to serve all kinds and sizes of congregations, this language has shifted and differed, so in every church I've had to learn how to preach to that particular congregation. Working alongside the church musicians, I have sought the best musical language to serve those people.

In Gail Godwin's novel *Evensong*, a young minister named Margaret Bonner is in training to be an Episcopal priest. She grows frustrated with her Clinical Pastoral Education course regimen. She writes an older priest she admires for advice and counsel. "How can I be sure this is my vocation?" she asks. He writes back, "Something's your vocation if it keeps making more of you."[10] Such is the promise of those for whom ministry in music, or any ministry, is vocation: it keeps making more of us!

Why and with what hope do we practice our vocation in leading worship? One of the simplest and most beautiful kinds of furniture is that of the Shaker community, a community whose daily motto is "Lift your hands to work and your hearts to God." The Shaker leader Sister Mildred says of those buying their chairs, "People don't see the chairs as a consecration." Yet this is what the monk Thomas Merton wrote of their furniture: "The peculiar grace of a Shaker chair is due to the fact that it was made by someone capable of believing that an angel might come and sit in it."[11] That's the way we do our work of worship—planning a worship space and environment with the belief that an angel might enter in!

Notes

1. David A. Cooper, "Invitation to the Soul," *Parabola* 9, no. 1 (February 1994): 9.

2. Frederick Buechner, "Vocation," in *Wishful Thinking: A Theological ABC* (New York: Harper &Row Publishers, 1973), 95.

3. Cooper, "Invitation," 9ff.

4. Brené Brown, interview with Richard Rohr, Brené with Father Richard Rohr on Spirituality, Certitude, and Infinite Love Part 2 of 2, Podcast audio, April 27, 2022, https://brenebrown.com/podcast/spirituality-certitude-and-infinite-love-part-2-of-2/.

5. C. S. Lewis, "On Church Music," in *Christian Reflections* (Grand Rapids, MI: Willam B. Eerdmans Publishing Co.,1967), 96–97.

6. Wendell Berry, "Profit in Work's Pleasure," *Harper's Magazine*, March 1998, 19–24.

7. Pablo Casals, *Joys and Sorrows: His Own Story as Told to Albert E. Kahn* (New York: A Touchstone Book, 1970), 105.

8. Casals, *Joys and Sorrows*, 135–36.

9. Casals, *Joys and Sorrows*, 60.

10. Gail Godwin, *Evensong* (New York: Ballantine Books, 1999), 12.

11. Thomas Merton, *Seeking Paradise: The Spirit of the Shakers* (n.p.), quoted in Cathy Newman, "The Shaker's Brief Eternity," *National Geographic* 176, no. 3 (September 1989): 309.

Chapter 13

The Song of the People of God

Worship the LORD with gladness; come into his presence with singing.
—Psalm 100:2, NRSVCE

. . . be filled with the Spirit, addressing one another in psalms and hymns and spiritual songs, singing and making melody to the Lord with all your heart . . . —Ephesians 5:18-19, RSV

The most important music in worship is congregational song. Augustine's oft-repeated words speak of its importance: "Whoever sings [to God in worship], prays twice." When we sing, we pray once with the words and then in the music, once with the mind and then with the heart. The spiritual effect is more than doubled; it brings the deepest soul to life.

The worship of the people of God—temple, synagogue, and church—is filled with song. Paul's words in Ephesians, a round-robin letter to all his churches, describe the marvelous variety of worship music: psalms, hymns, and spiritual songs. The early church was a singing church with a rich diversity of song. Let's explore the richness of these modes of congregational song.

Donald Hustad describes these three forms of worship song:

Psalms were historical, biblical and/or contemporary expressions of praise and prayer directed to YHWH; hymns were (at the time they were written) "Jesus songs" intended to express and to teach the basic doctrines of the new faith; and spiritual songs were highly emotional, spontaneous jubilations which occurred in the overpowering consciousness of the presence and power of the Holy Spirit.[1]

Hustad then describes how these three forms evolved and developed through the history of Christian worship:

PSALMS (whole psalms, that is) include all the forms of prayer: adoration and praise, of course, but more thanksgiving in recounting God's gracious acts, plus confession, petition, and even lament. HYMNS . . . express and teach faith, not only Christology, but all of theology . . . . And spiritual songs (with and without glossolalia) express the joy of our experience in Christ through the Holy Spirit.[2]

Using Husted's template, we see that there are New Testament examples of each form.

The Psalms formed the hymnbook of Jesus, which he adapted in various places, for example in his words from the cross (Psalm 22:1 and Psalm 35:1). The Hebrew canticles are reshaped and recited by Mary (the *Magnificat*), Zechariah (the *Benedictus*), and Simeon (the *Nunc Dimittis*) in Luke's birth narratives (Luke 1:47-49; 1:68-79; and 2:29-32). For the first decades of the life of the church, followers of Jesus worshiped in the temple singing the psalms of their faith.

The hymns of the early church were often vehicles of teaching theology and Christology. These Christological hymns of the New Testament include

• Philippians 2:6-11—The hymn to the Christ who emptied himself of divinity to come to earth as Jesus of Nazareth.
• Colossians 1:15-20—A hymn to the cosmic Christ present at creation.
• Colossians 3:14—A verse of an early baptism hymn.
• Revelation 4:8; 4:11; 5:12; 15:3-4; 19:1-8—Hymns to God and to the Lamb.

Finally, spiritual songs were the ecstatic, sometimes wordless songs. In 1 Corinthians, Paul writes about those who "sang in the

Spirit," perhaps a musical form of glossolalia, singing in tongues, and differentiated them from those "singing with the mind." He honors both kinds of worship singing (see 1 Cor 14:13-16).

In the first centuries of Christian worship, Christians sang the *jubilus*, which prolonged the singing of the last word, as in "alleluia," with joyful sound. St. Augustine wrote of the *jubilus*,

> It is a certain sound of joy without words . . . it is the expression of the mind poured forth in joy . . . . A person rejoicing in exultation, after certain words . . . bursts forth into sounds of exultation without words so that he . . . filled with excessive joy cannot express in words the subject of that joy.[3]

Modern worship has given us the gift of anthems, songs of worship that express, as John Calvin said of the Psalms, "all parts of the soul." In Appendix I, I include a list of anthems that have thrilled me through the years and that give expression to all parts of the soul and aid in all the movements of worship.

Psalms, hymns, and spiritual songs can also be voiced to the congregation through a vocal solo. The solo has been used in many church traditions across the theological spectrum. I've often enjoyed the way a vocal solo can introduce a congregation to musical genres beyond its usual repertoire, like the singing of the spiritual "Sometimes I Feel Like a Motherless Child" in a service planned to make room for lament; "Simple Song" from Leonard Bernstein's Mass for a unique song of praise; on Easter, from Handel's *Messiah*, "The Trumpet Shall Sound" or "I Know That My Redeemer Liveth"; or Gillian Welch's "Rock of Ages," which offers the congregation a jubilant way to experience a beloved hymn in new words and musical language.

As with all those who participate in leading worship, soloists must exercise spiritual caution, offering themselves to God and the congregation to facilitate true worship, not as a performance to elicit the applause of worshiper. As with those who offer prayer, a soloist ought not to express only the individual's experience but give voice to the whole body of God's people gathered to worship. Kierkegaard's model again guides.[4]

Soloists, ensembles, or choirs may sometimes wish to offer a piece of music from the secular world. Some people would question this, but I believe that music is made sacred by the God to whom it is offered. Words and music given to God, directed to God as an aid to the congregation's worship, can accomplish a sacred purpose.

How can we today best incorporate the rich variety of music in psalms, hymns, spiritual songs, anthems, and solos both ancient and new? Let us begin with the Old Testament book of Psalms. Psalms was the hymnbook of Jesus, and we have a rich hymnody that sets to music whole psalms or psalm paraphrases. Two beautiful examples are "Praise My Soul, The King of Heaven," a paraphrase of Psalm 103, and "My Shepherd Will Supply My Need," a paraphrase of Psalm 23.

In the summer of 2024, I was in Inverness, Scotland, and happened by the Scottish Free North Church as they were beginning a "Festival of Psalms." The singing of psalms, principally metrical hymns unaccompanied, is a part of their regular Sunday worship, and for this Saturday afternoon festival, the church was full to the balconies of worshipers joining together for more than an hour of full-throated, full-hearted singing. It was glorious. Several men, all in boisterous voice, took turns leading the singing of each psalm. At the end of each stirring psalmic hymn, a minister rose to the pulpit to introduce the next psalm and speak of its power. The order of worship of this marvelous afternoon is in Appendix II.

Old Testament psalms can aid our worship not only in song but as responsive readings at the beginning of worship. Psalms can be spoken or sung between the service's other Scripture readings, as practiced in historical liturgy. I have found particular beauty in listening to the psalms read in the "Grail" translation, used in monastic communities, as they are chanted back and forth, one group of monks to the other.[5] I have used this translation to aid responsive readings of the Psalms in worship.

For me, and for most Christians, hymnody is inseparable from the musical, theological, and spiritual treasure of the hymnbook. People worshiped God before printed hymnbooks, and people will worship God when hymnbooks are no more, but I regret the growing loss of the rich history of faith that is bound between each hymnbook's covers. They provide the church a "canon" of hymns that represent the best of hymnody through the centuries. The word "canon" is used often to talk about the sixty-six books of the Bible agreed on by the church to provide a measuring stick of God's revelation. It first referred to the sections of reeds that were used to measure everything. Like the biblical canon, the hymnal can give us a representative array of sacred hymnody.

In the Free Church tradition, every church must sing its worship of God according to the needs of the congregation and the leading of the Spirit. Today, hymns are sometimes printed in the bulletin, and in other churches they are projected on a screen. There are many and various ways of offering hymns to the congregation to assist in their worship of God and preserve the treasures of the great hymns of our faith.

We should also be heartened by a veritable explosion of new hymns and songs that serve the church in marvelous ways. Some of our best contemporary hymnals are including them. A list of some of these hymns are included in Appendix IV.

Now to spiritual songs, which include simple songs such as "scripture songs." I have heard them dismissed as "camp songs," but the singing back to God of the word of God can be a valuable form of worship. They are often easy for both adults and children to learn, which allows adults to put down the printed word and sing it by heart and allows children to sing along in worship. Scripture songs are also of great value as they allow us to incorporate children more fully into worship. As with any piece of music, spiritual songs can serve the meaning and movements of the worship service.

The diversity of spiritual songs available to us today is a great gift. From the Taizé community of France, we have received songs that repeat lines, often from Scripture, in a prayer-like way. Those in the Taizé community sing them as a way of merging their spirits with the spirit of God, and some American churches are incorporating them effectively. Western churches are also being introduced to the vibrant worship of churches in Africa and South America, surely one of the great gifts of our time.[6]

Psalms, hymns, and spiritual songs multiply in the worship of the church. The variety of song in worship expresses the abundance of God's marvelous world. Harold Best ended his 1999 address to the American Choral Directors Association, "Authentic Worship and Faithful Music Making," with these stirring words:

> Once we understand the underlying principles of authentic worship, then we are free to come back to the plethora, the richness, the beauty, and variegated delight of the works of worship. Now we are completely free; free of them, now free to offer them; free to see them disappear as incense, immediately lost in the overwhelming presence of the Lord himself; now free to study and draw from them. . . .
>
> Only then are we free, this will sound strange I know, to become small, powerless and weak again, knowing that the strength and power of God are made perfect in our weakness. Only then are we free to understand that true worship generates and welcomes true diversity, not because diversity is so "with it" . . . but because worship is so cosmically boundless, so fundamentally simple, and so God-intoxicated that we have no choice but to reach for the thousand tongues, knowing that no single tongue, no single style, no single order of worship, no single anything, can begin to capture the glory and the grace.[7]

Years ago, I was in San Francisco, where I saw an exhibit of Tibetan wall art, the Tibetans' equivalent of the stained-glass art of Western cathedrals. As I entered the last room of the exhibit, I saw that it was dominated by a large mandala on the floor, about eight feet in diameter. Composed of thousands of grains of colored sand, it was a stunning work of art. It was created over the course of months by Buddhist monks who had traveled to San Francisco from Japan. I learned to my astonishment that at the end of the exhibit, the mandala would be swept up and poured out in a sacred ceremony.

I realized this is what choirs do every week: they practice an anthem for hour after hour, and on Sunday morning they release it into the air, an offering to God and to the congregation, the sounds changing us and then disappearing from our hearing. And so it is with the organist and the pianist, and so with all the prayers, psalms, hymns, and spiritual songs lifted as incense to God. And so it is, I would add, the preacher's sermon after diligent hours of faithful work is offered to God and then to the congregation and then wafts away on the air.

Notes

1. Donald Hustad, "Doxology: A Biblical Triad," *Ex Auditu* 8, (December 1992):21

2. Hustad, "Doxology, 21–22.

3. Hustad, "Doxology, 20.

4. See Søren Kierkegaard, *Purity of Heart Is Willing One Thing* (New York: Harper Brothers, 1938).

5. See *The Psalms: Grail Translation from the Hebrew* (Chicago: GIA Publications, 2000); *The Psalms: A New Translation from the Hebrew Arranged for Singing to the Psalmody of Joseph Gelineau* (New York: Paulist Press, 1963). The newer publication seeks to make the psalms more inclusive in language but does not have the accent marks that aid the singing.

6. *Church Hymnary*, 4th ed. (Norwich: Canterbury Press, 2005). A rich treasury of historical hymns, Scottish hymns, and hymns from world Christianity and Taizé.

7. Harold Best, "Authentic Worship and Music Making," paper presented at ACDA National Convention, February 1999.

Chapter 14

Instrumental Music as a Sacrament of Praise

What I thank you for is simply this, that whenever I hear you I find myself set on the threshold of a good and orderly world, both in sunshine and in rain and by day and by night. (From an "Open Letter" to Mozart from twentieth-century theologian Karl Barth)[1]

Before there was the Word, there was the Sound. Then the Sound formed the Word. Can you remember the first sounds you heard? Was it the sound of your mother's heart beating rhythmically near your still-forming ears in the womb or the sound of the waters of the womb swirling around you those nine months of gestation? Did you hear your mother singing to you before you were born? I first heard sacred sound as a young boy sitting with my twin sister beside my mother in church. Have you heard a parent humming a hymn and felt its benediction? In early Hebrew worship, the first sound was and is today, on special holy days, the blowing of the shofar, the ram's horn. Then the congregation sings the Shema, the "Hear, O Israel" from Deuteronomy 6:4:

> *Sh'ma Y'Israel*
> *Adonai Eloheinu*
> *Adonai Echad.*
> Hear, O Israel!
> The Lord is our God.
> The Lord is One.

Sound, then the words of Israel's creed. Israel stands before God as a listening people. So after the *Shema* comes the greatest commandment:

"And you shall love the LORD your God with all your heart and with all your soul and with all your might" (Deut 6:5).

Worship often begins with instrumental music, in my tradition with the organ or piano. It begins in sound. This is most often expressive praise or sometimes a more contemplative praise that ends in a hush. Then, as the service moves along its path of worship, instrumental music guides our hearts to God: interludes before prayers, an offertory while the offering is taken, music not intended to cover the sacred action but to stir our hearts to devotion. At the end, the postlude sends us out with joy. I was sitting in the front pew at Broadway Baptist Church listening to Al Travis, our organist, play his "Toccata on Marion." As the music of the organ built, emotion began to rise in me, and at the climatic end I emitted an involuntary quiet yelp of joy.

Instruments introduce hymns and accompany choirs and soloists. What would we do without the sounds of instruments? The Hebrew psalms enumerate the instruments that help our praise and worship of God:

> Praise God with trumpet sound;
> praise God with lute and harp!
> Praise God with tambourine and dance;
> praise God with strings and pipe!
> Praise God with clanging cymbals;
> praise God with loud clashing cymbals!
> Let everything that breathes praise the LORD! (Psalm 150:3-6, adapted)

We praise God with clapping hands, not as applause but as adoration. We praise God with the human instrument of our body and with every other instrument we can find. We worship in sound, with sound, through sound without words. In ecstatic praise the words fall away into sound. We become one with God, a unitive experience as primal as those first sounds in the womb.

When the preeminent twentieth-century theologian Karl Barth died in his study, Mozart's "Magic Flute" was playing on the phonograph. Barth spoke and wrote many times about his appreciation for the music of Mozart and considered him no less than a theologian of creation. He said Mozart displayed in his music a knowledge of creation "in its total goodness" that few theologians had known. Mozart had heard, wrote Barth, ". . . the harmony of creation to which the shadow belongs but in which the shadow is not darkness, deficiency is not defeat, sadness cannot become despair . . . ." There is darkness in our world, but in Mozart's music, "the light shines all the more brightly because it breaks forth from the shadow." Barth "heard all creation enveloped by this light."[2] Instrumental music can give us the grace of peace and hope when we have no words.

Throughout the history of worship, there has been argument over the appropriate kinds of musical instruments in worship, from no instruments to a list of approved and disapproved instruments. The psalmist says bring them all! God loves all instruments! The criteria for instrumental music in worship are the same as for all acts of worship: Does it serve? Does it serve to bring the movements of our hearts to God? Does it aid in our jubilation, our thanksgiving and praise, our contemplation, our lament? Does it spur our hope and resolve?

Or does it reduce us to music consumers at a concert?

The human voice without words can be an instrument of worship. Humming, for example, or the call-and-response music of the older Black worship tradition can become the sounds of joy or lamentation, cries, groans and whispers like waves rushing over us. I was at a funeral recently, and as the old familiar hymns were sung, I began to hear someone whistling the hymns. It was his worship, and I was moved.

Sometimes words get in the way. Protestant worship can become overly, almost oppressively wordy. Instrumental music saves us, freeing us from words that can dominate worship. And what about silence? There is no music without silence, the quarter note rest, the half rest, the whole rest, then the hushed silence at the end of a piece of music. Our silence too can be praise. Liturgical theologian Gail Ramshaw recommends moments of silence at a number of places in the service: at the entry to worship, after the prelude, the prayers, the sermon, the benediction. Where in our lives do we make room to receive the gift of silence? Worship can be one of those blessed places.

I was writing a sermon I had named "A Tale of Two Cathedrals," a sermon that ponders the mystery of God's providence by comparing the fates of two British cathedrals during the bombing raids of World War II. One cathedral, Durham Cathedral, was spared when morning clouds obscured the bombing sites. In terrible contrast, Coventry Cathedral was utterly destroyed along with the entire city.

In the years after the war, Coventry Cathedral was rebuilt in striking new architectural form and has become an international center for peace and reconciliation. As I prepared the sermon, I listened to Samuel Barber's "Adagio for Strings," a piece that conveys both beauty and pain in its harmonies and dissonance. The music aided my writing of the sermon, and before I preached, I asked the organist to play the organ arrangement of the orchestral piece. The sounds conveyed the terrible beauty of the experience of those two cathedrals.

On a rainy day in London, I was taking in the art at the National Gallery Museum, and when I left, I hurried for cover in the nearest public building, St. Martin in the Fields. As I walked in, I heard music in the sanctuary. It was the oboe solo in the adagio movement in Marcello's *Oboe Concerto in D Minor*, a rehearsal for a chamber music concert that would be held later that night. Grace came to me in the wind and rain and the voice of the oboe.

At Myers Park Baptist Church on Palm Sunday, a special tradition ends the service. A massive cross, similar to the size of Jesus's own cross, is carried in somber recession from the sanctuary to the front lawn, where it is planted in the ground. The size of the cross, borne by women and men from the diaconate, conveys a sense of the danger of that day. As the procession begins at the chancel, the organist and violinist begin to play Albinoni's "Adagio." Holy Week has begun in our hearts, commencing with instrumental music.

Writer Anne Lamott describes a moment of her conversion that began at the end of a service in her predominantly Black church in Marin County, California, across from a flea market:

> The last song was so deep and raw and pure that I could not escape. It was as if the people were singing in between the notes,

weeping and joyful all at the same time, and I felt like their voices or *something* was rocking me in its bosom, holding me like a scared kid, and I opened up to that feeling—and it washed over me.[3]

I have felt this kind of feeling. It was the first Sunday after the terrorist attacks of September 11, 2001, and we staggered into worship. The first hymn with the brilliant improvisations by Paul Oakley, our Minister of Music and organist, brought us to God in renewed hope and faith: "A mighty fortress is our God, a bulwark never failing!" As the third stanza unfolded, "And though this world, with devils filled, should threaten to undo us," the organ sounded with the furies of darkness, but then the organ swelled with the words we needed to hear: "we will not fear, for God hath willed his truth to triumph with us!" And then the last line of triumph: "His kingdom is forever."[4] We were ready to go on.

When I was at Broadway Baptist Church, we conducted the memorial service of Rildia Bee Cliburn, the mother of Van Cliburn, who with his mother was a member there. Mrs. Cliburn loved to waltz. The Ft. Worth Symphony was there to play in the service. At one moment, they played Tchaikovsky's "Serenade for Strings." When do we hear songs in three-quarter time in worship? Not often—sometimes in hymns old and new. Then came the waltz movement. Is a waltz appropriate in worship? When that movement of the piece began, I looked down at Van Cliburn and saw a beatific smile span his face as he heard the music his mother loved and remembered her dancing. Only a waltz could have brought that moment. Yes, it is appropriate indeed.

When I help a family plan a funeral, one of the most important parts of the conversation is the kind of music they want, the music their loved one loved. Sometimes these are hymns, other times solos, but often, most movingly, a piano or organ playing a beloved song, a song without words touching the hearts of all who grieve that day. The burial service concludes as the casket of the deceased is lowered into the ground. A bugle plays taps. A bagpipe plays "Amazing

Grace." Our lives began in the sounds of God, and now in sound they return to God, our Maker, Lover, Redeemer, Friend.

Notes

1. Karl Barth, *Final Testimonies* (Grand Rapids, MI: Wm. B. Eerdmans Publishing Company, 1977), 19.

2. Karl Barth, *Church Dogmatics* 3, no. 1 (New York: T&T Clark, 1958), 297–99.

3. Anne Lamott, *Traveling Mercies* (New York: Anchor Press, 1999), 50.

4. Martin Luther, "A Mighty Fortress Is Our God," tune: EIN FESTE BURG, 1529, https://hymnary.org/text/a_mighty_fortress_is_our_god_a_bulwark.

Chapter 15

On the Recovery and Renewal of Congregational Singing

When we sing alone, we are led out of ourselves into the world of the song.
When we sing together we create a community, a communion in sound.
The group becomes more than the sum of its parts: it is creating beauty.
—Alice Parker[1]

Musick, alas! Too long has been
Prest to obey the devil....
Musick in Virtue's Cause retain,
Rescue the Holy Pleasure.
—Charles Wesley[2]

This is a time of both great excitement and great peril in congregational singing. The most important music in Christian worship is congregational song, and in some quarters hymn singing is on the wane. Following the direction of Dom Gregory Dix as cited in Chapter 2, singing in church should not primarily be something we watch but something we do. There is a "hymn renaissance" in the United States today and there is the demise of hymn singing in church.[3] However, in such times as these hymn singing can find rebirth, and that is the hope that drives this chapter.

What is a hymn? Gail Ramshaw begins with this definition, "metrical and imaginative congregational song," and goes on to broaden the discussion of what she calls "hymns of intelligent praise." In hymn-singing traditions, "hymns become central to the people's piety."[4] Hymns are a form of what Paul called "singing with the mind," but of course with more, the mind, heart and soul too. It is the intelligible singing that praises God, gives thanks to God, remembers God's acts of salvation and expresses all parts of the human soul brought before God. Hymn singing is a bodily act too. Richard Watson describes it as language in action: "The writing comes off the page, back into the body, lungs, blood."[5] So much of worship in many churches happens from the shoulders up and rarely from the shoulders down. All head, no body. We are not bodies with souls, we are souls with bodies, and our bodies want to worship too.

Charles Wesley led a revival in congregational song so to "rescue Holy Pleasure."[6] So we should set ourselves to the same pursuit. Hymn writer and theologian Brian Wren states that part of the problem we face is that our culture undermines our hymn singing with "performance-oriented popular music, electronic discouragement, and over-amplification."[7] Many worship spaces today copy performance halls. The floors are carpeted, the only sounds that can be heard are amplified sounds. The congregation can hardly hear themselves sing.

Yet, hymn singing is so vital in our worship of God! Brian Wren outlines the hallmarks of congregational song. First, it is "corporate." We sing together as the Body of Christ, all members of one another in the Christ's Body. The congregation becomes, in the words of William Lock, ". . . a Spirit-filled organism which acts with one heart, mind and voice."[8]

Secondly, it is "corporeal," that is, a whole-body experience. God made us as God made Jesus as embodied beings, not "brains walking on stilts." We stand, we sing, we sway, bodies in action as we offer ourselves to God, the first audience of our singing.

Thirdly, it is inclusive. We all sing together. Some better than others, but it doesn't matter. Make a joyful noise, and any sound you can make. A man who might be called today in modern parlance "an uncertain singer" said to Wren:

I need to sing. . . even though I don't know when I'm on key. . . .But singing is important to me. When I'm in a crowd with others, I can sing from my heart, and not worry about how it sounds."[9]

The question is not, so Donald Hustad, "Do you have a voice?" But, "do you have a song?"[10] These words from poet Joan Walsh Anglund were put on a 2015 postage stamp: "The bird doesn't sing because it has an answer, it sings because it has a song."[11] What a song we've been given to sing!

Fourthly, it is "creedal." Wren describes congregational song as "creedal" in "a believing response in a self-committed way."[12] As so, it includes praise, thanksgiving, lament, trust and commitment. . . ." Our creeds become worship as we sing them. So too our theologies voiced in our hymns.

Fifthly, it is "ecclesial." It is the song of the church, "an acted parable of community." It voices the aims of the people of God and who they hope to be.[13]

Sixth, it is "inspirational." It lifts us out of ourselves. It helps us breath with God's own breath, as the word "inspiration" means.

Seventh, it is "evangelical". It can introduce the unbelievers, the outsiders to Christ. Donald Hustad, who taught church music at the Southern Baptist Theological Seminary in Louisville, Kentucky, and before that was the musical director for the Billy Graham Crusades, writes,

> It serves to proclaim the gospel to the uncommitted, as well as to witness to the experience which is available in Christ. It demonstrates the love relationship of the children of God and tends to reach out to with 'arms of melody' to include those who are not already a part of the church."[14]

I would add an eighth: "ecumenical." Hymns bring to us the hymns of the church around the world and through the centuries. As Gail Ramshaw puts it, "The church's collection of hymns are an ecumenical treasure." She goes on, "Hymns also open our narrow present to the hundreds of years of piety that went before us." As such, the "hymns of the past can free us from the prison of ourselves."[15]

In our age that puts our vaulted contemporary apprehension of the truth above the accumulated truth of the past, we must be reminded that while sometimes the present can free us from the shackles of the past, the past can free us from the blinders of the present.

Which brings us to the hymnbook. Traditionally the hymnbook has preserved the canon of the best hymns of the past and joined them with contemporary hymnody that brings to us in freshness the needs of the contemporary worship of the people of God. Unfortunately, the hymnbook is disappearing from the pews. The reasons are many, for example, hymns and songs regularly projected on a screen or printed in a bulletin, extensive use of congregational song outside the church's hymnal, and desires to change the words of hymns to be more inclusive. The aims may be good, but the hymnbook is relegated to the storeroom.

The problem with the loss of hymnals is the ideal of the hymnal as a "canon" of representative hymns that pass along the hymn tradition of the worship of the church is lost. Another, the idiosyncratic wishes of the pastor and minister/director of music may hold sway, less guided by the treasure of the hymnal. And this, when the pastor/music ministry staff leave, the church may be cast adrift on how to move along. A strong Worship Board/Committee, which I encourage in all churches, can lessen the impact of staff change.

Now to worship songs and songbooks. There is more than one kind of congregational singing. Brian Wren helps us by describing them with my own added examples. Here is his compendium:

Hymn: A sequence of stanzas, able to develop a theme and reach a conclusion. An example, "Praise, My Soul, the King of Heaven" (Henry Lyte 1834; John Goss 1869)

Chorus: A short song that states a theme without developing it—for easy singing, repetition and "uplift." Examples: "Sing Them Over Again to Me, Wonderful Words of Life (P.P. Bliss 1874) and "We Are Marching in The Light of God" (Siyahamba 2013)

Round: A type of chorus, giving the effect of a part-song. Example: "What Does the Lord Require of You?" (*The Faith We Sing* 2001, 2174.)

Refrain: An end-of-stanza chorus summarizing the message of the congregational song. Examples: "Leaning on the Everlasting Arms" (Elisha Hoffman, 1887), "Blessed Assurance, Jesus is Mine" (Fanny Crosby 1873), "Softly and Tenderly Jesus is Calling" (Will D. Thompson 1880).

Chant: Music permitting a text not written in verse to be sung by the congregation. Examples, chanting the Psalms and the Taizé chanting of scripture verses.

Ritual Song: A short congregational utterance that moves the action of worship, such as a song on the way to take Communion, or leading into prayer. Example: "Put Peace into Each Other's Hands and Like a Treasure Hold It" (Fred Pratt Green 1989).

Spirit Singing: Improvised congregational singing, usually based on a major chord. We also include singing in tongues.[16]

The resources for this kind of congregational song are plentiful. A number of denominational hymn committees have published hymn supplements, smaller and less expensive song books that offer a wider variety of congregational song, e.g. *The Faith We Sing*. I also recommend *Common Ground: A Song Book for All the Churches*, which includes a number of songs and hymns of the Iona Community and is immensely singable. Appendix V lists exemplary hymn books and song books.

Considering hymn lyrics. Brian Wren offers this guidance. They should be "devout," meaning devoted to the worship of God. They then are God-centered, focusing on serving God alone, and praising, glorifying, and delighting in God, the Living One.

The second criterion is "just." To love our neighbors includes treating them justly and fairly, in action, speech and song." "A just lyric," Wren writes, "will not reinforce cultural stereotypes of age, and gender."

The third is "frugal," an economy and simplicity of lyric. It avoids showy language that draws attention to itself. A Scottish preacher of years past gave this outline to his sermon on "The Prodigal Son: Sick of Home; Homesick; Home." A model of such simplicity in hymn lyrics is: "God of the Sparrow, God of the Whale."

The next is "beautiful." Beautiful lyrics are pleasing to the senses, they are lasting, and they partake of the beauty of God manifest in the world. Here is beauty in service to the worship of God. The Psalmist leads us: "O worship the Lord in the beauty of holiness (Ps 29:2, KJV). Beauty is one of pathways of God into our lives.

The next, as discussed above, is "communal". They bring the congregation together as one. They should be understood by the whole so by their nature do not exclude.

The next to last is "purposeful." It serves the purpose for its use in worship.

And the last is "musical." It "wants" to be sung, to be put to music. It should be easy enough to sing for most of the worshipping congregation and doesn't discourage the singer. Who wants a hymn as difficult to sing as the American National Anthem?![17]

Now to the difficult, sometimes vexing, problem of altering hymn texts either by a hymn book committee or a minister/director of music in a local congregation.

Some believe we should never change the lyrics to hymns. A variety of reasons are given. But the words to hymns have been changed forever! The founder of English hymnody, Isaac Watts, wrote in the preface to his *Hymns and Spiritual Songs*: ". . .what is provided for public worship should give to sincere consciences as little vexation and disturbance as possible." Then adds, "where any unpleasing word is found, he that leads worship may substitute a better; for we are not confined to the words of any Man in our public solemnities."[18]

So how shall we make changes? Brian Wren defines "acceptable change" with these words:

> Individual reactions to lyric changes depend on how far they disturb the singer's memory bank, how far the reason for change is understood and accepted, and how elegantly the changes are made."[19]

Sometimes the changes come when old archaic words have lost or changed their meaning. In Charles Wesley's wonderful hymn on the Jacob story, "Come, O Thou Traveler Unknown," the last stanza went:

> "To me, to all, thy bowels move,
> Thy nature and thy name is love." (1742)

In today's *United Methodist Hymnal*, the lyrics go:

> "To me, to all, thy mercies move—
> thy nature and thy name is Love." (387)

Oft times today the call to revise is inclusive language for God and the people of God. One of my favorite hymns is "Praise, My Soul, The King of Heaven." The lyrics are a hymn paraphrase of Psalm 103. The 1834 lyric by Henry Lyte begins with this stanza:

> Praise my soul the King of heaven,
> To his feet your tribute bring.
> Ransomed, healed, restored forgiven,
> Evermore His praises sing.

(then, like the waves of the ocean):

> Alleluia! Alleluia!
> Praise the everlasting King!"

The third stanza has been changed to address the issue of inclusive language. The 1834 lyric by Henry Lyte went:

> Father-like, he tends and spares us;
> well our feeble frame he knows.
> In his hands he gently bears us,
> rescues is from all our foes.
> Alleluia! Alleluia!
> Widely yet his mercy flows.

The *United Methodist Hymnal* has altered the text in the most helpful and beautiful way:

> Father-like, God tends and spares us;
> well our feeble frame God knows;
> mother-like, God gently bears us,
> rescues us from all our foes.
> Alleluia! Alleluia!
> Widely yet God's mercy flows.

The changes are important, but they are not jarring. We can sing them without disturbance or vexation.

Ruth Duck, one of our most skilled hymn writers, has altered hymn text in an admirable way in *The Chalice Hymnal*. Here is her stanza three alteration:

> "Mother-like God tends and spares us,
> knowing well our fragile frame.
> Father-like God gently bears us,
> Tender- hearted, slow to blame.
> Alleluia! Alleluia!
> All within me praise God's name![20]

Wren's guidance of lyric changes is helpful for all worship language, not just in hymns (see below in the chapter on worship language, "The Color of Water—Worship Language for Everyone").

Now to the ways we can improve hymn singing. We begin with the keen desire to improve it, valuing it at least as much as other forms of worship music. This requires diligent worship planning time on how to do so.

I have spoken about the acoustics of the sanctuary that aid not inhibit congregational song. Completely carpeted worship spaces inhibit hymn singing. If a church is renovating the sanctuary they should consider, for example, carpeting only the aisles. Some churches are making acoustical choices that help the streaming of services to the detriment of those who are actually worshipping there on Sunday. The ideal is a worship space where, if possible, given the size of a sanctuary, the unaided voice of a worshipper or of a small children's choir can be heard without amplification.

One more suggestion comes from the incomparable Alice Parker who is unparalleled in leading congregational song. In her article, "How Can We Sing Without the Organ," she recommends the singing of one unaccompanied song each Sunday.[21]

I've been in worship where one stanza of a hymn has been sung without instruments and it was a soul stirring experience. Parker writes that unaccompanied singing helps the congregation find its own voice! The purpose of congregational song is not "art," she writes, but "the building of community through song."

There is an amazing treasure of new hymns being written. A hymn festival in church could mix old and new hymns. A church could choose one new hymn a month and teach the congregation to sing it. Or, as for beloved older hymns, the congregation could be given a hymn survey revealing their ten favorite hymns, and the worship leaders could make more use of them more than once a year, or when the texts and themes call for them.

The holy need of people to sing together deserves the best work of ministers, church musicians and worship committees. As church attendance and hymn singing have declined, there has arisen other opportunities for the need of people to sing together, for example, evenings where people can come together and sing a Broadway musical, like *South Pacific* or *The Sound of Music*. Let us

then in our worship renew our hymn singing, and so with Charles
Wesley, "rescue holy pleasure"!

Notes

1. Alice Parker, *Melodious Accord: Good Singing in Church* (Chicago: Liturgy Training
Publications, 1991), 115.

2. Charles Wesley, "The True Use of Music," quoted in Brian Wren, *Praying Twice: The
Music and Words of Congregational Song* (Louisville, KY: Westminster John Knox
Press, 2000), 387.

3. Russell Schultz-Widmar, "The Hymn Renaissance in the United States," in *Duty and
Delight: Routley Remembered* (Norwich: Canterbury Press, 1985), 191-216.

4. Gail Ramshaw, *Words That Sing* (Chicago: Liturgy Training Publications, 1992), 2-3.

5. J. Richard Watson, "The English Hymn," quoted in Brian Wren, *Praying Twice: The
Music and Words Congregational Song* (Louisville, KY: Westminster John Knox Press,
2000), 82.

6. Wren, *Praying Twice*, 387.

7. Wren, *Praying Twice*, 53.

8. Wren, *Praying Twice*, 85.

9. Wren, *Praying Twice*, 89.

10. Donald Hustad, "Doxology: A Biblical Triad," *Ex Auditu* 8, (December 1992).

11. The quote, often attributed to Maya Angelou, is found in Joan Walsh Anglund, *A
Cup of Sun* (n.p., 1967).

12. Wren, *Praying Twice*, 90.

13. Wren, *Praying Twice*, 93.

14. Donald P. Hustad, *Jubilate II* (Carol Stream, Illinois: Hope Publishing Company,
1981), 383.

15. Ramshaw, *Words That Sing*, 3-4.

16. Wren, *Praying Twice*, 191-252.

17. Wren, *Praying Twice*, 175-188.

18. Wren, *Praying Twice*, 297-8.

19. Wren, *Praying Twice*, 306.

20. Daniel B. Merrick, ed., "Praise My Soul, the God of Heaven," in *Chalice Hymnal*
(St. Louis: Chalice Press, 1998),23.

21. Alice Parker, "How Can We Sing Without the Organ?" *NewSong—Brian Wren
Newsletter*, no. 10 (September 1993).

Part 4

Issues in Worship Today

"My God, thou art a literal God, a God that wouldst be understood literally and according to the plain sense of all that thou safest; but thou art a figurative, a metaphorical God too; a God in whose words there are such a height of figures, such voyages, such peregrinations to fetch remote and precious metaphors, such extensions, such spreadings, such curtains of allegories, such third heavens of hyperboles, such harmonious elocutions, . . .thou art the Dove that flies." —John Donne[1]

Note

1. John Donne, "XIX Expostulation," in *Devotions Upon Emergent Occasions* (Ann Arbor: University of Michigan Press, 1959), 124.

Chapter 16

Prayer in Worship, Worship as Prayer

. . . then patch
a few words together and don't try
to make them elaborate, this isn't
a contest but a doorway
into thanks, and a silence in which
another voice may speak.[1]

We could call worship itself a "school of prayer." It teaches us how to pray. This chapter is about prayer and its various expressions in worship.

We've looked in previous chapters at the ancient formulation of the church, *lex orandi, lex credendi*, the law of prayer and law of belief, or doctrine. Does prayer flow into doctrine, or does doctrine inform and direct prayer? Our own prayers and the prayers that permeate our worship reveal to us that it is not either/or. The interplay between the two is crucial. Prayer in worship involves the whole person, mind, heart, and life and thus may be the living heart of our theology.[2]

As we think about prayer in worship, we must consider that there are some key polarities at work. The first is the polarity between what have been called "prayers of expression" and "prayers of empathy." Prayers of expression are the free, unhindered prayers of the heart. The rabbinic tradition tells a story to illustrate its importance: There was once a shepherd boy who prayed every night under the stars, "Master of the Universe, I would tend your sheep for free even though I tend others' sheep for pay, because I love you!" One day a learned rabbi came by and scolded the boy for praying such an unschooled prayer.

So he taught the boy some of the great prayers of the faith like the Shema, the "Hear, O Israel," and left.

Later, the rabbi was awakened by a dream where a Voice said, "You have robbed me of the prayers of one of my favorite children!" Disturbed, the rabbi rushed back to find the boy. Finding him, he said, "I have heard you are not praying anymore!" The shepherd boy answered, "Yes, this is true. You forbade me to pray the prayer I was praying, and I forgot the ones you taught me." At which point the rabbi said, chastened, "Go back to praying the prayer you were praying."

Our spiritual lives need these prayers of expression that flow from our hearts, uncensored and free. They come in our private worship and also in public worship as we silently whisper them between the notes of the songs and lines of the liturgy. And in some church worship, people are invited as moved by the Spirit to offer these prayers to God in the midst of the people of God.

The second kind of prayer, prayers of empathy, are the guided prayers of the people of God in worship. There is a rabbinic story for this form of prayer too. A small European village had one clock-maker. He died, and for a while there was no one to take his place. Things were fine for a while, but then the villagers' clocks began to run fast or slow. Some kept winding their clocks because, as they reasoned, a clock that ran erratically was better than no clock at all. Others, however, stopped winding their clocks. What good is an inaccurate clock?

After a long period of time, a new clockmaker arrived in the village. He announced, "Tomorrow at dawn, I will be in the town square to repair your clocks." At dawn the next day the people lined up. But this is what the clockmaker discovered: for those who had stopped winding their clocks, the workings had rusted, and he could not fix their clocks; but for those who had kept their clocks wound, the workings were in good shape, and he could repair their clocks.

The moral of the story is that we need to come to worship and pray with others, sometimes using the set prayers of the faith. Such regular praying can help us keep our spiritual life alive. In times when our spirits are dry, the expressive prayers of the heart may cease, but if we are faithful in joining the church in praying and prayers, our spiritual lives can yet find sustenance.

The Anglican *Book of Common Prayer* is spiritual treasure of prayers prayed throughout the worship service, prayers that guide our souls into God's presence and guide our hearts in the spiritual life. I have also found the Presbyterian and Methodist books of worship a great help in private devotion and public prayer in worship. This oft-quoted prayer by Thomas Merton, American monk and spiritual writer, is the sort of prayer that can be used in worship to help the bewildered and spiritually unsure bring themselves to God:

> My Lord God,
> I have no idea where I am going. I do not see the road ahead of me. I cannot know for certain where it will end. Nor do I really know myself, and the fact that I think I am following your will does not mean that I am actually doing so. But I believe that the desire to please you does in fact please you. And I hope I have that desire in all that I am doing. I hope that I will never do anything apart from that desire. And I know that if I do this you will lead me by the right road, though I may know nothing about it. Therefore will I trust you always though I may seem to be lost and in the shadow of death. I will not fear, for you are ever with me, and you will never leave me to face my perils alone.[3]

In Free Church worship, prayers can be set prayers or free prayers. Free Church worship has used three kinds of prayers to different degrees: (1) Set Prayer, as found in a worship book and perhaps printed in the worship bulletin; (2) Free Prayer, prepared beforehand in the words of the one praying; and (3) Extemporaneous Prayer, prayer spontaneously offered as guided by the Spirit. Earnest extemporary prayers offered to God alone can guide our hearts in prayer.

Another polarity to consider is what we might call "open-eyed" prayer and "closed-eyed" prayer. Open-eyed prayer uses all the senses to know God and praise God: sight, taste, smell, touch, and hearing. God comes near to us as we take in the world God has given us. Beauty is a pathway of the Lord into our lives. Poet Edna St. Vincent

Millay begins a sonnet on the glories of fall with words that are a kind of open-eyed prayer: "O World, I cannot hold thee close enough."[4]

"Closed-eyed" prayer is not about squinching up our eyes with the kind of instruction given many years ago as we entered into prayer: "Every head bowed; every eye closed." Rather, it happens when we let the world fall away so we can be with God in a still heart and still mind. The ways of the world have crowded our lives during the week, and now we set them aside. The words of the poet William Wordsworth become ours:

> The world is too much with us; late and soon,
> Getting and spending we lay waste our powers;
> Little we see in Nature that is ours;
> We have given our hearts away, a sordid boon.[5]

So we let the world fall away as we pray.

There are prayers that praise, prayers that thank, and prayers that ask. Then there are prayers where we simply abide in God and invite God to dwell in us. This is "Prayer as Being." On the wall of the Quiet House at Laity Lodge in Texas, in hand-stitched letters is this arrangement of the words of Psalm 46:10:

> Be still and know that I am God
> Be still and know that I am
> Be still and know
> Be still.
> Be.

Now we address another polarity not only of prayer but of theology and spirituality too, named in the mystical tradition of the church, *kataphatic* and *apophatic* spirituality. *Kataphatic* spirituality is also called the *Via Positiva*, or the Positive Path. It means "with the face" and is based on the God we can see and know. It uses images, words, metaphors and all the senses as a pathway to God or as a pathway of God to us. These are all windows open to God.

Apophatic spirituality is about the God beyond our knowing. It is called the *Via Negativa*, or the Negative Path. It means literally "without a face." Negative here does not carry a bad connotation as we commonly think of the word but means that which is unknown. The *Via Negativa* leads us to confess our not knowing of God. We view God as holy mystery. We let go of words, symbols, metaphors, and images. These are no longer adequate. Gail Ramshaw says mystical apophatic spirituality uses "God-is-not" language.[6] The mystic Pseudo-Dionysius urges us to let God be God rather than forcing God into our categories. The medieval mystic Meister Eckhart said to his students, "Now pay attention: God is nameless, because no one can say anything or understand anything about him. . . . So be silent and do not chatter about God; for when you do chatter about him, you are telling lies and sinning."[7]

Good theology, and therefore good prayer, lives between what we know about God and what we cannot know about God. It is willing to live in a state of not knowing, which is what the word "agnostic" means. We have both a God who has revealed God's self and a God hidden, beyond our knowing, called by some *Deus absconditus*. Without apophatic spirituality, we can easily make an idol of our own thoughts, ideas, symbols, and images—an idol of our theology.

St. John of the Cross wrote of this experience of not knowing as the "dark night of the soul." In such times, we dwell in what the anonymous medieval English writer called "the Cloud of Unknowing." Times like these can lead to a new and more adequate faith. The poet John Keats described a creative state of mind that he called "Negative Capability" where someone ". . . is capable of being in uncertainties, Mysteries, doubts, without any irritable reaching after fact & reason."[8] By leading us into the not-knowing, the *Via Negativa* can lead us to a new awareness of God.

How can our prayer and worship give expression to both kinds of spirituality? Most Western worship is based on *kataphatic* spirituality. But here are some ways we can allow apophatic spirituality into worship. First, our prayers can confess what we do not know and so help us bow before the mystery of God. One such prayer might begin, "O God beyond our knowing, our seeing . . . ."

Our worship can become too wordy! We need more silence and fewer words. As Henri Nouwen said, "We expect too much from talking and too little from silence."[9] Silence in worship can leave room for us to dwell in the God beyond our knowing and seeing. In the ancient temple worship of the Hebrew people, there were no images on the altar in order to preserve the Mystery of God and protect against any form of idolatry in image or mind. Are the altars of our worship ever bare?

Poet and spiritual writer Kathleen Norris says her best prayers are the ones she doesn't understand. She says to God, "I mean this prayer even though I don't know what I mean."[10] Hymns can help us here:

Immortal, Invisible, God only wise,
In light inaccessible, hid from our eyes.[11]

"Who is like Thee?" the psalmist cried. And reverence answers, "No one, nothing!" All our words, images, and symbols come up short. God is the Holy One beyond our best thoughts, words, and songs.

Now I will address the leading of prayers, the saying of prayers, and the writing of prayers. First, public prayer is not private prayer made public. Approaching prayer this way makes it too easy for prayers to become so individualistic and personal that they do not lead us to God but rather reduce listeners to onlookers of the spirituality and personal life of the person praying. "Lord, I've had a hard week, but you have been with me" may be true for the one praying but may not serve to help the congregation offer their prayers. Again, Kierkegaard's model of worship serves us: the role of the one leading prayer is to help the people say what they most need to say to God in prayer. Our worship traditions offer prayers refined over the years, prayerfully composed to help us bring our whole selves to God.

As for the writing or composing of prayers, the opening Collect of Anglican worship can be our guide.[12] Not only can it serve as a template as we seek to write our prayers for public worship, but it can also guide our private prayer lives as well. Writing a prayer can be a helpful spiritual exercise.

The Address: "*Almighty God.*" Now our hearts and minds are focused on God.

The Description of God: *". . . unto whom all hearts are open, all desires known, and from whom no secrets are hid."* We cannot take in the totality of God any more than we can take in the Atlantic Ocean at a glance, so we offer one specific glimpse of who God is that describes why we are praying now.

The Petition: *"Cleanse the thoughts of our hearts by the inspiration of thy Holy Spirit."* We voice the particular petition of the prayer as needed at that part of worship.

The Dedication of Life: *". . . that we may perfectly love thee and worthily magnify thy holy Name."* We cannot pray sincerely to God without offering of ourselves to God with a readiness for God's transforming and guiding presence.

The Ascription: *". . . through Jesus Christ our Lord."* Praying in Jesus's name is praying in the Spirit of Jesus and his way. It is a way of saying with Jesus, "Not my will but thine be done."

The Amen. "So let it be!"

Regarding extemporaneous prayers in worship, the one praying should spend time praying alone as they prepare to pray publicly. Yes, Jesus says, the Spirit will give us utterance, the right words for the present hour, but the prayerful planning of public prayers does not preclude the guidance of the Spirit as one prays. I urge ministers to train and teach laypeople about the meaning and purpose of public prayer, including the worship goals of each kind of prayer. Otherwise, it is too easy, for example, for the Invocation to become whatever the person praying wants it to be.

Honesty and humility require us to remember that in all praying, we say with Paul, "Likewise the Spirit helps us in our weakness, for we do not know how to pray as we ought, but that very Spirit intercedes with groanings too deep for words" (Rom 8:26). We cannot even pray to God without God. So we pray, "O Holy Spirit, would you sort out and translate what I'm trying to say in this prayer to God?" No matter how weak and stumbling our prayers, God is listening to the sighs and whispers of our hearts. So, as we prepare to pray in public worship, we say, "God, I need your help on this!"

One of the most beautiful forms of praying in the Spirit is praying in tongues, as practiced in the Pentecostal stream of Christianity. This form of Spirit-led prayer can happen as one prays in a private room or in public worship as everyone is invited to pray at the same time. A mother in one of my churches had a young son who was born with a fatal liver disease. It could not be cured. The only issues were how long he would live and what medical treatment he should receive. The mother, who was not a Pentecostal, told me that she did not know how or what to pray and that praying in tongues had been a gracious gift to her.

Prayer is where "deep calls to deep" (Ps 42:7). May our worship prayers be such prayer.

Notes

1. Mary Oliver, "Praying," in *Devotions: Selected Poems of Mary Oliver* (New York: Penguin Press, 2017), 131.

2. See Geoffrey Wainwright, *Doxology* (New York: Oxford University Press, 1980), 218–83. See for an excellent discussion of these matters.

3. Thomas Merton, *Thoughts in Solitude* (New York: Farrar, Straus & Giroux, 1978), 103.

4. Edna St. Vincent Millay, "God's World," in *Renascence and Other Poems* (New York, Harper & Brothers, 1917).

5. William Wordsworth, "The World Is Too Much with Us," in *The Norton Anthology of English Literature*, vol. 2, rev. ed. (New York: W.W. Norton & Company, 1968), 160–61.

6. Gail Ramshaw, *Reviving Sacred Speech: The Meanings of Liturgical Language; Second Thoughts on Christ in Sacred Speech* (Akron, OH: OSL Publications, 2001), 28.

7. Ramshaw, *Reviving Sacred Speech*, 29.

8. John Keats, "To George and Thomas Keats, December 21, 27 (?), 1817," *Selected Poems and Letters*, ed. Douglas Bush (Boston Houghton Mifflin Company, 1959), 261.

9. Henri J. M. Nouwen, *The Genesee Diary: Report from a Trappist Monastery* (New York: Doubleday, 1976).

10. Roy Kelleher, "Kathleen Norris," *Poets and Writers Magazine* 25, no. 3 (May/June 1997),71.

11. Walter C. Smith, "Immortal, Invisible, God Only Wise," tune: ST. DENIO, 1867, https://hymnary.org/text/immortal_invisible_god_only_wise.

12. *The Book of Common Prayer* (New York: The Seabury Press, 1979), 323.

Chapter 17

Wintry and Summery Spirituality—Worship for All Seasons of the Heart

John Calvin called the book of Psalms "the anatomy of all parts of the soul." Indeed, it is. The psalms help us bring all parts of the soul to God: praise, thanksgiving, trust, confession, lament, anger, rage, longing, fear, and doubt. We tend to use the more upbeat and comforting psalms in our worship, but we do so at the neglect of parts of our souls. We need to bring all of what we are to God, not just our "church selves" but our real selves, not just our acknowledged selves but also our disinherited selves, so we may receive the healing we most need. This goes beyond allowing space in our worship services for lament, as discussed in chapter 5. Bringing all of what we are to God involves affirming our own and each other's true selves, true natures, and the nature of our spiritual lives—on Sunday and every day.

Let's start with "wintry and summery spirituality." In our current church era, we tend to promote the latter and neglect the former. Church historian Martin Marty introduced to me the concept of two kinds of spirituality: summery spirituality and a "wintry sort of spirituality." It was the 1980s, and Marty, having suffered the death of his beloved wife, was walking through a wintertime of the spirit. He wrote movingly of it in his book, *A Cry of Absence: Reflections for the Winter of the Heart.*[1] He began, "Winter is a season of the heart as much as it is a season of the weather." He found solace and help in Roman Catholic theologian Karl Rahner's typology of two kinds of spirituality—wintery and summery—and in Rahner's affirmation that each type has its own integrity and its own spiritual gifts to offer.

Summery spirituality lives in the warm immediacy of God's presence. It feels God, finds God, sees God everywhere. Joy fills its days. Some of us in my spiritual tradition grew up singing summery songs with lines like these: "There's within my heart a melody," "Every day with Jesus is sweeter than the day before," or "There's joy, joy, joy, joy, down in my heart." Later we sang, "Joyful, Joyful We Adore Thee," "All Creatures of Our God and King" with its rolling alleluias, or "For the Beauty of the Earth." Some people have that kind of spiritual happiness all their lives. They have felt the nearness of God often. Some children experience what German theologian Dorothee Soelle calls "childhood mysticism," a oneness with God, and it pervades their lives.[2]

Some experience summery seasons of their lives when all seems right and good. Life shimmers with light and joy. Summery spirituality can be a lifelong home with God, or it can be ours in certain times of our lives. Jesus said that he came so we might have joy and have it in fullness (John 10:10), and spiritual joy, which is a fruit of the Spirit, can and should be part of our weekly worship experience.

In contrast, wintry spirituality often lives with a sense of God's absence—what some call *deus absconditus*. Has God absconded with our faith? Paul says, "we walk by faith, not by sight" (2 Cor 5:7), by which he means walking without the feeling of faith. Some wintry Christians feel like they are out in a snowstorm looking in through a window. They see people inside by a fireplace, all warm and cuddled up together, and wonder why they are on the outside in the cold.

Some people are wintry types by nature. They stand a bit at a distance from life, observing and analyzing. We need them. They lead with their brains rather than their hearts. When others talk of "Jesus in my heart," or when they hear conversion stories like John Wesley's, who felt that his heart was "strangely warmed," wintry types may long for that, but such an experience is not theirs. They may wonder if something is wrong with them, whether their spiritual life is out of kilter.

But wintry spirituality has its own integrity and its own gifts, to offer the church and world. Theologian Joseph Sittler has confessed to being a wintry sort of Christian in his sermon "The View from Mount Nebo." At the end of Moses's life, although he had led the Hebrew people out of slavery in Egypt, through forty years of wandering in the wilderness, and finally to the edge of the promised land, he was told by God, heartbreakingly so, that he could not enter the promised land with his people. He could only view it from afar, from the top of Mount Nebo. In his sermon, Sittler recognized that there are those who sing "Blessed Assurance, Jesus Is Mine" out of their own experience, yet he acknowledged that there are others. Of them he wrote,

> Who knows what goes on in the hearts of men who lack the grace of adoration, of passion, of immediate blessed assurance, who lack full knowledge of God, who must live out their lives in hard, dutiful obedience to cooler graces because their lives are unattended by the hotter ones?

These people's Christian lives, he said, "are given, rather, to discernment, critical work, the effort to achieve a precise description of what is really involved in becoming and being a Christian."[3]

Moreover, there are those for whom all spiritual assurances and once-bedrock theologies are gone, and there is no knowing how long that test of faith may last. Perhaps someday a new and more adequate faith will come to them, but now it is winter, and it is night. The church needs to acknowledge and honor the people of both wintry and summery spirituality. For some churches, it is summer all the time. But can church be a place where all people can bring not only their unhindered joy but also their sadness?

The book of Psalms is such a place, welcoming all parts and all seasons of the human soul. If many churches are leaving their songs of lament unsung, they also seem to be ignoring the psalms of lament as well, those in which the psalmist calls out, "Out of the depths I cry to you, LORD" (Ps 130:1), or

How long, O LORD? Will you forget me forever?
How long will you hide your face from me?
How long must I bear pain in my soul
and have sorrow in my heart all day long? (Ps 13:1-2)

Dr. Tony McNeill, a national leader in Black church worship and music, writes, "I hope you are thinking critically about ways to create space for lament, grief, doubt, disappointment. . . ." He then offers these words of guidance: "Don't rush or bully people into praise. Let people be human in the ways they are designed to be." These are some of his suggestions for congregational songs that help us bring our sadness, doubt, and disappointment to God:

• "Pass Me Not O Gentle Savior"
• "I Need Thee Every Hour"
• "Standing in the Need of Prayer"
• "Come Ye Disconsolate"
• "Lift Every Voice and Sing"
• "Precious Lord, Take My Hand"
• "I Know Who Holds Tomorrow"[4]

There is another season of the heart. We might call it autumnal spirituality. It is the season of longing: longing for God, for love, for our real home. In his classic *The Varieties of Religious Experience*, William James explored the varieties of religious types and sects.[5] We are not all the same in our experience of God and need of God. Many people inhabit the season of autumnal spirituality.

Susan Cain explores this experience in her book *Bittersweet: How Sorrow and Longing Make Us Whole*.[6] Cain describes the bittersweet state or sometimes season of the soul as ". . .the tendency to states of longing, poignancy, and sorrow; an acute awareness of the passing of time; and a curious piercing joy at the beauty of the world."[7] Joy, longing, and beauty are all wrapped up together.

Advent is preeminently the bittersweet season, the season of longing for God and for peace, justice, and love. Psalm 42 is the epitome of an Advent psalm:

As a deer longs for flowing streams,
so my soul longs for you, O God.
My soul thirsts for God, for the living God.
When shall I come and behold the face of God?" (Ps 42:1-2)

We help autumnal people feel a sense of belonging as we give voice to this combination of longing and joy and beauty. We do so when we sing hymns that long for heaven and the completion of all things. The Adagio movements in symphonies often express this spiritual place inside.

Writing on faith in Hebrews, the author offers us words that speak "autumn." "All of these died in faith," he says, "without having received the promises, but from a distance they saw and greeted them. They confessed that they were strangers and foreigners on the earth" (Heb 11:13). Autumn people are part of our congregations every week. They feel homesickness, an exile, and we stand alongside them. The thirteenth-century mystic Meister Eckhart wrote, "God is the sigh of the soul." In worship, we leave room for sighs.

When I was at Crescent Hill Baptist Church, Grady Nutt, who lifted the spirits of the congregation every week, died in a tragic airplane crash. The grief of the congregation was enormous. He was a nationally known humorist and a regular on the TV show *Hee Haw*. On the day of his funeral, the sanctuary was packed with people from all over the nation, including *Hee Haw* actors and musicians.

At one moment in worship, Darrell Adams, a singer in the congregation, stood with his guitar and began to sing in his plaintive, clear voice the words of "In the Sweet By and By": "There's a land that is fairer than day, and by faith we can see it afar."[8] Someone from the *Hee Haw* crew began to sing with him, then more and more, until by time of the refrain all were softly singing, "In the sweet by and by, we will meet on that beautiful shore." Sorrow and longing and hope all blended into a moment of healing.

We've spoken about the importance of validating our laments and griefs and longings, but what about our feelings of anger and rage? There are psalms for that too, what some call "imprecatory psalms," like Psalm 109:

Do not be silent, O God of my praise.
For wicked and deceitful mouths are opened against me . . . .
In return for my love they accuse me,
even as I make prayer for them. . . .
They say, "Appoint a wicked man against him;
let an accuser stand on his right. . . .
May his days be few, may another seize his position. . . .
May the creditor seize all that he has;
may strangers plunder the fruits of his toil. . . .
For he did not remember to show kindness
but pursued the poor and needy
and the brokenhearted to their death."

Then the psalmist turns the hurt and hate over to God:

But you, O LORD my Lord,
act on my behalf for your name's sake. . . .
Help me, O LORD my God!
Save me according to your steadfast love. (Selected verses)

The psalmist owns his rage, then relinquishes it into God's hands.

Our hurt may be personal, or it may express our anger over the plight of the poor and vulnerable in our nation. I have used this psalm with people who have come to me in my office, overcome by hate they do not wish to feel. As we read it together, we have laughed and cried. We cannot let go of our hurt and hate unless we own it. Our feelings are not wrong; we have been wronged. People around us are being wronged. We acknowledge this and offer it to God.

How can we bring our hurt and hate to God in worship? Certainly, through the use of such psalms in worship, though we should not stop there—the healing of the gospel must also be heard, perhaps in the sermon of the day.

Worship is also where we voice our trust in God. The most beloved of the psalms are psalms of trust, like Psalm 23: "The LORD is my shepherd; I shall not want." Or Psalm 55:22: "Cast your burden on the LORD, and he will sustain you."

Then there are psalms that help us bring our fear to God. Fear can lock us in its prison. We can live, as someone has said, "locked in a room with open doors." Out of fear we do things we would not do otherwise. So we have this psalm: "The LORD is my light and my salvation; whom shall I fear?" (27:1). And this one:

> God is our refuge and strength,
> a very present help in trouble.
> Therefore we will not fear, though the earth should change,
> though the mountains shake in the heart of the sea . . . . (46:1-2)

There are times when we feel that the world has utterly changed. Things are shaken. *Terra firma* is no longer "*firma*"! We need these psalms, to read them and sing them.

The psalms are the anatomy of all parts of the soul. So should we bring all parts of our souls and every season of our hearts to God in worship. Let us bring all we are all the way to the altar.

Nineteenth-century evangelist Billy Bray said in his memoir, "I can't help praising the Lord. As I go along the streets, I lift one foot up and it seems to say, 'Glory'; I lift the other, and it seems to say, 'Amen!'"[9] As we come to worship, let us say Glory, Thanks, Help, Woe, Wow, and Amen.

Notes

1. Martin Marty, *A Cry of Absence: Reflections for the Winter of the Heart* (San Francisco: Harper & Row, 1983).

2. Dorothee Soelle, *The Silent Cry: Mysticism and Resistance* (Minneapolis, Minnesota: Fortress Press, 2001), 9-17.

3. Joseph Sittler, "The View from Mt. Nebo," in *Preaching the Story*, ed. Edmund A. Steimle, Morris J. Niedenthal, Charles L. Rice (Philadelphia: Fortress Press, 1980), 43–51.

4. Tony McNeill, "Music & Worship Leaders: I hope you are thinking critically about ways to create space," Facebook, November 7, 2024, https://www.facebook.com/tony. mcneill/posts/pfbid02vCZSMSJ1Ah2xjfbXtvpU2ueEZ4E8BXqoeWTca3h2Rf1WG-1ZtEanLpdX1DyHoPx6Al.

5. William James, *The Varieties of Religious Experience: A Study in Human Nature* (London: Longmans, Green and Co., 1928).

6. Susan Cain, *Bittersweet: How Sorrow and Longing Make Us Whole* (New York: Crown, 2022).

7. Cain, *Bittersweet*, xxiii.

8. Sanford Fillmore Bennett, "In the Sweet By and By," tune: SWEET BY AND BY, 1868, https://hymnary.org/text/theres_a_land_that_is_fairer_than_day_an.

9. Annie Dillard, *Pilgrim at Tinker Creek* (New York: Harper's Magazine Press, 1974), 271.

Chapter 18

The Color of Water— Worship Language for Everyone

How shall we find you,
God Who is Holy,
captured by gender, color and code?
How shall we worship,
God of the Presence,
action and essence, meaning and mode?[1]

In his memoir *The Color of Water*, award-winning novelist James McBride tells of a conversation he had with his mother one Sunday on the way home from church. He grew up in New York City, the son of a White mother and Black father. They lived in a Black neighborhood, and McBride went to a predominantly white school, so the issues of race and identity were large in his young mind. Large too, in his boyhood mind, was the question of the color of God. So, as they drove home from church that Sunday, he asked his mother, "Is God black or white?" She answered, "God is the color of water."[2]

How many colors are in water? All of them. With her answer, McBride's mother preserved the mystery of God. As water in mists and rainbows displays the full colors of the light, so must our language in worship seek to display the full glory and mystery of God.

As we and all the cosmos were brought into being by the Speaking of God, in worship we seek to return the best speaking we have to God. There is symbol, ritual, and music but also, crucially, speech. As the word "worship" itself means "worth-ship," what is the language of worship worthy of our God? Today, as we worship, we seek a language that is faithful, biblical, reverent, emancipatory, and inclusive.

In our day, few issues are more important and more embattled than those of worship language. Winston Churchill said, "We shape buildings; thereafter they shape us." So it is with the language of worship. I've found the most helpful liturgical scholar on language in worship to be Gail Ramshaw. In her brilliant work *Reviving Sacred Speech*, she says that the metaphors of the liturgy "transform us and our perception of and vision for the world."[3] The liturgy of the church through the centuries has been a sacred dance of preservation and creativity, conservation and innovation. "Liturgy," writes Ramshaw, has been "continually reworked so the ancient metaphors can speak God's mercy to us in a contemporary tone of voice."[4]

The challenge before us is set. People coming to worship hunger for words that open up and preserve the mystery of God, words for God and the people of God. God's people need to be set free from the language of the past that diminishes God and all people, words that are, as hymn writer Shirley Erena Murray phrases it, "captured by gender, color, and code."[5]

At the Iona Abbey off the coast of Scotland, people come to worship from all over the world and from a multitude of Christian traditions. The last time I worshiped there, the worship leader began as part of the welcome to worship, "We are very aware that, over time, language changes and there can be times, especially in prayers and songs, when we feel uncomfortable with it. As you sing or pray, feel free to make changes that make sense to you, in a respectful way." Those words help welcome all who come for worship.

In the beloved Lenten hymn "O Sacred Head Now Wounded," we sing these poignant words, a question: "What language shall I borrow to thank thee dearest friend?"[6] All language about God is borrowed from the ages, from those who have worshiped God over thousands of years, from the earth and sky. Creation sings God's glory. "Glory be to God for dappled things," exults the poet.[7] Language is a "borrowed light" as the moon borrows its light from the sun. Or, to use a Buddhist image, it is the finger pointing to the moon, not the moon itself.

Worship language is human language and therefore partial. How can we use language that helps and does not hinder our worship of God? Our worship language at its best points beyond itself so that at moments in worship even the words fall away. But revelation is bound up in speech. How then can our language be reverent, liberating, less idolatrous, and inclusive? How can it be welcoming to all who have come to worship so all feel that they belong? How can it be faithful?

Perhaps the first question is, "Is our worship language faithful?" For me, the answer to that question begins with asking, "Is it biblically faithful?" But what does that mean? The Bible teems with imagery of God that is inclusive, reverent, and emancipatory. However, we too often play one octave of the Bible or even only one note. When we do so, biblical words and images can be reduced to an idolatrously small number of words and images. So let our worship language be biblical, yes, but not slavishly so, not unreflectively so.

The Bible is itself a worship book, rich in the ways biblical people have worshiped through the centuries. It shows us how to praise, how to kneel in reverence, how to sing, and how to pray. The Bible contains more worship than doctrine. Its poetry and songs and stories feed our hearts and minds that hunger for God. Gail Ramshaw writes that doctrine is a "third-order" language, after the first-order speech of exclamation to God and the second-order speech of the narrative of our relationship with God.[8] In worship, we praise God, and we recall God's marvelous works and deeds. Then, afterward, theologians compose their theology and doctrines.

In some churches, we get only a small measure of the revelation of God in Scripture. The Old Testament prophet Amos warned of famine, not of food but of the word of God, and he said that when the word becomes scarce, we will not even know what we are hungering for (Amos 8:11-12). To be faithful to the Bible is to use the Bible in its full measure in all of worship, not just in the readings but at other moments—such as a fuller use of Psalms, which was the prayer book, songbook, and worship book of Jesus, Israel, and the church through the millennia. The Hebrew name for the book of Psalms is "The Book of Praises." We sing the great psalm paraphrases in hymns like the Scottish metrical psalms. We can also use Paul's great prayer in Ephesians as a prompt for our own prayers. I've found that the three-year Revised Common Lectionary helps us use the Bible in fuller measure throughout worship, not just in the snippets sometimes used for the preacher's sermon.

Now we turn to language in worship that speaks reverence. God loves every prayer we pray, but in public worship we seek language that conveys reverence for God. It can become too chummy with God, too casual, too chatty. But worship language can also be too stilted, and we can use older language with no currency of understanding. So Ramshaw recommends vernacular speech over colloquial speech.[9] Vernacular speech is the common tongue of a culture. It helps us understand the ancient tongue of worship traditions, and it avoids theological jargon. A woman in a former church rolled her eyes at me regarding ministers who use words like "eschatological" in worship. "Lord, we give you thanks for the eschatological horizon that brings us hope!"

As we address God, how ought we to name God and picture God? Ramshaw writes about metaphor as the heart of sacred speech. It brings two things together not normally joined to create a new experience, like the metaphor "ship of state." "God our rock" is a metaphor, as is "God our mother," "God our fortress," and "God, a nursing mother," as pictured in Psalm 131. Jesus use metaphors in the parables he told to teach something new about God and the kingdom of God, often in startling ways. The word parable means "to throw alongside." In his parables, Jesus threw the kingdom of God alongside our everyday world so we might imagine what the kingdom was like and what it would be like to enter it, to live in that realm of God's justice and joy, mercy and love. Metaphors work in worship. They help us imagine something new.

Reverent speech about God must then use many names and many images of God. Multiplicity preserves mystery. Brian Wren's hymn "Bring Many Names" is exemplary here.[10] When we reduce images and names of God to one or a few, we invite idolatry, making our own image of God a "graven image" in our minds and hearts. Even imitating Jesus's use of the word Father, or *Abba*, can become idolatrous if that is our sole language about God, as we let our cultural meanings of "father" distort the *Abba* to whom Jesus prayed.

How shall we speak God's Name? An early name for God among the Hebrew people was *El Shaddai*, which literally meant "God of Mountain Peaks" but is most often translated as "Almighty God." Translations, however, are always interpretations, and sometimes, as the old saying goes, "the translator is a traitor!" For our Living God, we need a living language, and we need fresh metaphors for God, as old names and old metaphors may hinder our worship more than help.

Out of an utter reverence for God scarcely comprehensible to us moderns, the Hebrew people refused to speak the holy Name of God given to Moses at Mt. Sinai. The four Hebrew consonants, YHWH, classically represented that name. Later, scribes added the vowels in between: YAHWEH. The name is a verb, translated variously, "I Am Who I Am," "I Cause to Be What I Cause to Be," or "I Am Who Was and Am and Shall Be." Out of reverence for the Name, Jews substitute the Hebrew word *Adonai*, which means Lord. But in this process of translation, we have taken name of God, which was a verb, and made it a noun referring to a male authority figure. A theological conference had as its title "God Is a Verb." It was a healthy reminder of who God is.

What should we do about this? Ramshaw offers the best translation of Yahweh I know: "The Living One,"[11] a translation that represents the verb-like character of the Name. It avoids both gendered language and hierarchical language. Some have traced the elemental nature of the name "YAHWEH" as coming from the sound of breathing: Ya, breath in, Weh, breath out. God has breathed life into us, and we breathe God's name back out into the world.

There is also the name Jesus used for God: *Abba*, the Aramaic word a babbling Hebrew child said for the father, like daddy or poppa. Every one of the nine prayers Jesus prayed that are recorded in the Gospels, except for one, began with *Abba*. The Abba experience of Jesus, his experience as the beloved son in whom God took delight, was at the heart of his spirituality. *Abba* conveyed intimacy, trust, confidence, and obedience. The only recorded prayer Jesus prayed without using the *Abba* address was his cry of desolation from the cross when he quoted Psalm 22: "My God, my God, why have you forsaken me?" And yet later came his last prayer, "*Abba*, into your hands commit my spirit." (Luke 23:46).

Paul wrote that the Spirit enables us to pray *Abba* with the same intimacy, trust, and confidence of Jesus's praying. Why does our worship so often neglect *Abba*, Jesus's name for God? We could easily pray and sing it in a way that enlarges and softens the connotations of the word "father" and signifies the nature of the God Jesus worshiped, a perfectly loving, compassionate, and trustworthy God. Theologian John Cobb has brilliantly explored the meaning of Jesus' Abba in his book, Jesus' Abba: The God Who Failed.[12]

How many ways are there to name Jesus? Jesus's Hebrew tradition expanded the meaning of God as Savior far beyond the most common one—that of saving us from our sins. To the Hebrews of Jesus's time, "Savior" also meant the toppling of tyrants and the healing of the world. Today we often use "Christ," which means "Messiah" or "Anointed One." And we use "Lord" perhaps most often. Thomas's confession as the risen Christ appeared to him, "My Lord and my God," has led the way in that name (John 20:28). Yet, while "Lord" connotes the one to whom we give our ultimate loyalty, it is more than the title of a male authority figure. Ramshaw's suggestion of "Living One" as a helpful translation of YHWH is also a fine translation of Jesus, the Lord, the Living One, risen to partake in the divine life of God and in our lives today. We should also consider that in some Christian traditions, in Black and evangelical worship, the title "Lord" may not connote merely a male authority figure but is often an affectionate and intimate form of address: "Dear Lord, my sweet Lord, precious Lord."

Welsh poet Waldo Williams describes the coming of Jesus, then and now, and uses these images: the outlaw, the huntsman, the lost heir, the exiled king, and the one who escapes conscription of every army. How this sparks our imagination of how he might come in the world today![13]

Jürgen Moltmann raises an important question: Are there names or titles for Jesus that do not reinforce our male, hierarchical cultural arrangements? For example, the three main Christological categories used in Christian theology for Christ have been Prophet, Priest, and King. Moltmann offers another Christological title, "Jesus the Friend." Using Jesus's words to his disciples, "I call you not servants but friends," and his opponents' jeering words, "a friend of tax collectors and sinners," Moltmann offers a title that brings Christ close alongside us and speaks grace to us today.[14]

But there are many more names by which we can know Jesus. Islam speaks of the "Ninety-Nine Names of God" as a way of honoring the mystery of God and rejoicing in God's splendor. If we looked through the centuries of Christian worship, spirituality, and theology, we could come up with our own Ninety-Nine Names of Jesus, A to Z, including "Jesus the Center," "Jesus, My Great Dignity," and "Jesus our Mother," and "*Ihidaya*," the early Syriac Church's name for Jesus that means the "Whole One" or "Unified One."[15] For Jesus, as for God, "bring many names!"[16] Yes, "O for a thousand tongues to sing my great Redeemer's praise!"[17]

Now let us consider emancipatory language in worship. Emancipatory language sets us free from various forms of cultural and political enslavement. During the 200-year period of chattel slavery in America, slave owners distributed to their slaves a highly truncated version of Christian Scripture, the "Slavery Bible," a version that kept in all the passages used to justify slavery and excised the parts that might start rebellion. Our own worship language has also been curated to put down social unrest and protest, as when the King James Version of the Bible, authorized by the king of England, replaced instances of the word "tyrant" with the word "king."

In Alice Walker's modern classic *The Color Purple*, Shug, a young black woman who has suffered sexual abuse, talks about trying to pray: "Whenever you trying to pray, and man plop himself on the other end of it, tell him to git lost . . . . Conjure up flowers, wind, water, rock." She was trying "chase that old white man out of her head" as she prayed.[18] So should we all.

Emancipatory language frees us from the cultural norms that can rule our lives. Harry Emerson Fosdick's great hymn, "God of Grace and God of Glory," is resplendent with emancipatory language.[19] Black spirituals are full of emancipatory language, with the language coded with hidden meanings that white masters would not understand. For example, language about heaven was code for the road to freedom in the here and now. What language in our modern worship diminishes the worth of some people in the community? Abandon it or change it.

All of the above leads us to the important, sometimes contentious issue of language about God and the people of God, which is gendered, androcentric language. A child might ask if God is a man. But isn't God beyond our notions of male and female? Beyond gender? Years ago, a woman came to me to talk about her beloved brother who had transitioned to be a woman. Sometimes she referred to her brother as "he," other times as "she." At one point she broke into tears and said, "Pronouns are so hard!" Yes, they are, and we will stutter and stammer for a time before we figure out the most caring, respectful, and inclusive way to use pronouns in worship language. If we do it right, we might help others outside the church who are also struggling with these issues.

To reflect together on the holy name of God is to enter into a serious conversation about the nature of the God we worship. As we consider resolving the issue of exclusively male and patriarchal images of God, we can begin by being at least as inclusive as the Bible is, making use of the feminine images of God in Scripture, such as God as a nursing mother in Psalm 131, a psalm I call "Theology as Lullaby." In Hosea 11, God is pictured as a mother grieving over her wayward child. Hosea describes God as a mother who nursed her child, Israel, taught her to walk, raised her, and now has watched as her child wandered afar. "How can I hand you over, O Israel?" God cries (v. 8). We also have a maternal image of Jesus, weeping over Jerusalem, who said, "Jerusalem, Jerusalem . . . How often have I desired to gather your children together as a hen gathers her brood under her wings, and you were not willing!" (Matt 23:37-38). God is beyond male and female and yet partakes of both male and female.

Mystics like Julian of Norwich wrote of God as Mother and Jesus as Mother: "As truly as God is our Father, just as truly is he our Mother." Inspired by this description, William Mathias has written a stunning anthem for choir and organ: "As Truly as God Is Our Father" (1987).

Bobby McFerrin, the musical genius who came to fame with his pop song, "Don't Worry, Be Happy," and who has been the visiting conductor at major American symphonies, has composed a spiritually revelatory choral anthem, "The 23rd Psalm." McFerrin changes every "he" of this beloved psalm to "she" ("She maketh me to lie down in green pastures . . .") so that by the end of this incantatory anthem, we are somehow, some way, changed.[20]

The change in metaphors has altered the way we picture God and the world. I close with Ramshaw's call and invitation:

> I urge: always open it up, open it up. Open the Bible, to see what images mean. Open up the tradition, and find there Christian riches long forgotten, religious jewels locked up in dusty chests. . . . Open up the memories of conservative grandparents, for whom the traditional imagery conveyed mercy. Open up the creativity of newfashioned writers, who can share with others fresh metaphors of mercy. Open it up, open it up. By the power of the Spirit, life not death, will enter and grow.[21]

Notes

1. Shirley Erena Murray, Hope Publishing Company, 1995.

2. James McBride, *The Color of Water: A Black Man's Tribute to His White Mother* (New York: Penguin Publishing Group, 2006).

3. Gail Ramshaw, *Reviving Sacred Speech: The Meaning of Liturgical Language* (Akron, OH: OSL Publications, 2000), 13.

4. Gail Ramshaw, *Reviving Sacred Speech*, 13.

5. Shirley Erena Murray, Hope Publishing Company, 1995.

6. Arnulf and Bernard of Clairvaux, "O Sacred Head Now Wounded,", tune: PASSION CHORALE, 1656, https://hymnary.org/text/o_sacred_head_now_wounded.

7. Gerard Manley Hopkins, "Pied Beauty," in *The Poems of Gerard Manley Hopkins* (Oxford: Oxford University Press, 1967), 69.

8. Ramshaw, *Reviving*, 2.

9. Ramshaw, *Reviving*, 3–4.

10. Brian A. Wren, "Bring Many Names," in *Bring Many Names* (Carol Stream, IL: Hope Publishing, 1989), 9.

11. Ramshaw, *Reviving*, 64.

12. John Cobb, *Jesus' Abba: The God Who Has Not Failed* (Minneapolis, Minnesota: Fortress Press, 2015).

13. Waldo Williams, "Between Two Fields," quoted in Rowan Williams, *The Poems of Rowan Williams* (Oxford: Perpetua Press, 2002), 92–93; Rowan Williams, *Open to Judgement* (London: Darton, Longman & Todd, 1984), 131.

14. Jürgen Moltmann, *The Church in the Power of the Spirit* (New York: Harper & Row, 1975), 114–21.

15. See my own list in H. Stephen Shoemaker, *Jesus Stories* (Valley Forge, PA: 2016), 205–207.

16. Brian A. Wren, "Bring Many Names," tune: WESTCHASE, (Carol Stream, IL: Hope Publishing Company, 1989), https://hymnary.org/text/bring_many_names_beautiful_and_good.

17. Charles Wesley, "O for a Thousand Tongues," tune: AZMON, 1739, https://hymnary.org/text/o_for_a_thousand_tongues_to_sing_my.

18. Alice Walker, *The Color Purple* (New York: Washington Square Press, 1982), 179.

19. Harry Emerson Fosdick, "God of Grace and God of Glory," tune: CWN RHONDDA, 1930, https://hymnary.org/text/god_of_grace_and_god_of_glory.

20. "The 23rd Psalm," track 12 on Bobby McFerrin, *Medicine Music* Blue Note Records, 1990.

21. Ramshaw, *Reviving*, 81.

Worship and the Moral Life

Yes, there is beauty and there are the humiliated. Whatever may be the difficulties of the undertaking, I should like to never be unfaithful to either one or the other. —Albert Camus[1]

Neo-Hasidic scholar Arthur Green captures the moral dimension of worship as he writes, "The 'pleasure' God takes in human worship needs to be understood in terms of the human goodness and love brought forth in the worshipper and in the human community."[2] His words echo the prophetic critique of worship that we find in the Old Testament prophets.

In the New Testament, Jesus is asked, "Teacher, which commandment in the law is the greatest?" Combining two texts from his Hebrew Scriptures, Jesus answers, "'You shall love the Lord your God with all your heart and with all your soul and with all your mind.' This is the greatest and first commandment. And a second is like it: 'You shall love your neighbor as yourself'" (Matt 22:36-39). Those are our two loves—our love of God and the love we offer our neighbor. They bring together the subject of this chapter: Worship and the Moral Life.

In all four Gospels, Jesus joins the prophetic critique of Hebrew worship. Through the voices of the Old Testament prophets, God makes it clear that the ethical/moral life of the nation has to be one with their worship life. And God did not hold back. Let's take Amos first, the pincher of sycamore trees who was called by God to preach God's justice and righteousness to the northern kingdom. He showed up at the royal sanctuary at Bethel on the high holy day of the nation when all were gathered to celebrate the northern kingdom, an event as important as a combination of a president's Inauguration and July 4th in Washington, DC. As Amos called the nation to account, he began with a set of denunciations of the nations surrounding Israel. The "amens" filled the air. Then he began reciting the sins of Israel!

> Thus says the LORD:
> . . . they sell the righteous for silver
> and the needy for a pair of sandals—
> they who trample the head of the poor into the dust of the earth .
> . . . (Amos 2:6-7)

Next, he turned to the religious leaders of Israel and the comfortably pious and thundered:

> I hate, I despise your festivals,
> and I take no delight in your solemn assemblies.
> Even though you offer me your burnt offerings and grain offerings,
> I will not accept them . . . .
> Take away from me the noise of your songs;
> I will not listen to the melody of your harps. (5:21-23)

Finally, he proclaimed what God *does* want:

> But let justice roll down like water
> and righteousness like an ever-flowing stream. (5:24)

The prophets declared that justice and righteousness were two sides of the same coin. God wants social justice *and* personal righteousness. God wants just laws that protect the weakest *and* individual morality, like telling the truth and not cheating your customers. The prophet Micah began his critique of worship with a question:

> With what shall I come before the Lord,
> and bow myself before God on high?
> . . . with burnt offerings

. . . with thousands of rams, with ten thousands of rivers of oil?
Shall I give my firstborn for my transgression . . . ? (Mic 6:6-7)

Then he answered,

He has told you, O mortal, what is good,
and what does the LORD require of you
but to do justice and to love kindness,
and to walk humbly with your God? (6:8)

Sidney Harris, a columnist in the 1960s and 1970s, wrote in his
sardonic way, "God could do well with less praise from his followers
and more imitation." These prophets would agree.

Jesus echoed Micah and the prophets in his denunciations of the
religious leaders of his day: ". . . you tithe mint, dill, and cumin and
have neglected the weightier matters of the law: justice and mercy
and faith" (Matt 23:23). Quoting Hosea, he said, "Go and learn
what this means, 'I desire mercy, not sacrifice'" (Matt 9:13).

In the New Testament, Paul addresses problems in the Corinthian church, whose observance of the Lord's Table neglected simple
care for poorer members of the congregation. In the weekly love
feast before the sharing of the bread and cup, the wealthier members
would shove themselves to the front of the line and gorge themselves
with food, leaving the poorer members at the back of the line with
little left to eat. Paul did not mince words: the wealthy members
were humiliating those who had nothing and so profaning the Lord's
table (see 1 Cor 11:17-22). And in the book of James, the writer
confronts favoritism toward the rich and the dishonoring of the poor
in congregational worship (see Jas 2:1-7).

How does the prophetic critique of worship in the Bible challenge us to think about the moral dimension of our own worship?
Liturgical theologian Don Saliers at Candler School of Theology
has addressed these important matters at length over his career as a
teacher. For him there is a vital connection between worship and the
moral life. He writes,

The relations between liturgy and ethics are most adequately formulated by specifying how certain affections and virtues are formed and expressed in the modalities of communal prayer and ritual action. These modalities of prayer enter into the formation of the self in community.[3]

As discussed previously, theologians often ponder the meaning of the relationship between *lex orandi* and *lex credendi*, the law of prayer and the law of belief. As we believe, so we pray, or as we pray, so we believe. Worship and its prayers are a deep expression of belief, but Saliers borrows one more phrase as essential, adding *lex vivendi*, the law of living.[4] The Hebrew prophets would say, "Yes! How we live is the deepest expression of what we believe!"

When Saliers writes of worship as shaping the "affections," he is speaking of the deepest places of our being, where mind, heart, and spirit join. In his Jefferson Lecture, "It All Turns on Affection," Wendell Berry spoke of affection as the key to all good work. Berry held that religious morality alone is not sufficient for moral progress:

> The *primary* motive of good care and good use [of the earth] is always going to be affection, because affection involves us entirely. . . . Without this informed practical and *practiced* affection, the nation and its economy will destroy the country.[5]

In our deepest places, worship shapes our moral and ethical lives.

For Saliers, the essentials of worship are praise, thanksgiving, and the retelling and reenacting of the central narratives of the faith and God's acts of salvation. Liturgy shapes the moral life, yes, but he warns, "When liturgy is regarded primarily as a means of moral exhortation or ethical instruction, it loses its essential character as praise, thanksgiving and anamnetic enactment of the mystery of faith."[6] Without praise and affection, the preacher can become a moral scold, and worship can be purely didactic.

With that warning in mind, let's examine how worship can shape the moral life. We begin with the preacher and the texts. The sermon is the most direct way the worship service addresses the ethical life of God's people. I've heard preachers say, "I'm not an Old Testament prophet; I'm a New Testament evangelist," drawing a distinction Jesus never made. It is all too easy for a minister to let their own predilections determine the choice of texts in order to avoid moral and ethical teaching, even when using the texts of a lectionary.

I think many ministers wish to balance their preaching between pastoral sermons and prophetic sermons. I can sympathize. No congregation needs a wire brush of a sermon every week! One might, then, avoid preaching from the book of James with its exacting moral teaching or postpone a series of sermons on the Ten Commandments (all ten—one cannot pick and choose!). We need also to bear in mind that we are speaking of morality that is broader than sexual morality. Dorothy Sayers was once lecturing on the Seven Deadly Sins. Someone came up to her before the lecture and asked, "What are the other six?"

Another way to think about ethical teaching and preaching is to follow, as discussed earlier, the rabbinic tradition of biblical commentary that combines both *Halakah* and *Haggadah*. *Halakah* centers on the ethical and moral teaching in the Scriptures, while *Haggadah* centers on the narratives. Both form character. And, as mentioned earlier, they are often placed beside each other in Scripture, one following directly after the other, story first and then ethical teaching.

Now we turn to the liturgy, the songs and prayers of the worship service. In Don Saliers's essay "Liturgy and Ethics: Some New Beginnings," he writes strikingly of how the prayers of worship shape our character. Prayers of praise and thanksgiving place us in a good world given to us by God and dispose us to deep gratitude. They remind us of who God is and how God has acted and now acts toward us and the world. Prayers of confession acknowledge how we have fallen short of the mark of God's righteousness and our own deepest values. Prayers of lament express our sorrow over the waywardness of the world. Prayers of intercession ground us in the reality of the deep needs of the world and in the love of neighbor whose welfare is linked to our own, reminding us that we are all bound up together in reality as it is.[7]

Along with sermons and prayers, hymns, too, form the moral life, like the nineteenth-century hymn "Dear Lord and Father of Mankind" or the twentieth-century hymn "God of Grace and God of Glory." They help us confess our moral foolishness and poorness of soul as they call us to our best.

The fabric of biblical faith is built on indicative threads of what God has done and is doing for us and the world—"Your sins are forgiven"—and imperative threads of biblical commands—"Go and sin no more." "You are the light of the world," an indicative, is followed by the imperative ". . . let your light shine before others, so that they may see your good works and give glory to your Father in heaven" (Matt 5:14, 16). In worship, the moral life of God's people is shaped by the God who saves *and* commands. This is how God's people worship biblically!

In *Doxology*, Geoffrey Wainwright writes of the moral life in worship:

> Into the liturgy the people bring their entire existence so that it may be gathered up in praise. From the liturgy the people depart with a renewed vision of the value-patterns of God's kingdom, by the more effective practice of which they intend to glorify God in their whole life.[8]

Those words sum up not only this chapter but the whole book. And now for the concluding hymn:

> Set our feet on lofty places;
> fill our lives that we may be
> strengthened with all Christ-like graces
> pledged to set all captives free.
> Grant us wisdom, grant us courage
> lest we fail our call from Thee,
> lest we fail our call from Thee.[9]

Notes

1. Albert Camus, "Return to Tipasa," in *Camus: Selected Essays and Notebooks*, trans. P. Thody, (Scottsdale, AZ: Peregrine Books, 1970).

2. Arthur Green, *Judaism for The World: Reflections on God, Life, and Love* (New Haven: Yale University Press, 2020), 13.

3. Don Saliers, "Liturgy and Ethics: Some New Beginnings," in *Liturgy and the Moral Self: Humanity at Full Stretch Before God*, ed. E. Byron Anderson and Bruce T. Morrill (Collegeville, MN: Liturgical Press, 1998), 17.

4. Saliers, "Liturgy and Ethics," 4.

5. Wendell Berry, "It All Turns on Affection," in *It All Turns on Affection: The Jefferson Lecture and Other Essays* (Berkeley: Counterpoint, 2012), 32–33.

6. Saliers, "Liturgy and Ethics," 33.

7. Saliers, "Liturgy and Ethics," 19–22.

8. Geoffrey Wainwright, *Doxology: The Praise of God in Worship, Doctrine, and Life (A Systematic Theology)* (New York: Oxford University Press, 1980), 8.

9. Henry Emerson Fosdick, "God of Grace and God of Glory," in *Chalice Hymnal*, (St. Louis, MO: Chalice Press, 1998), 464.

Part 5

The Spiritual Practice of Planning and Leading Worship

Chapter 20

Sacred Time— The Seasons of the Church Year

"So hallowed and gracious the time." —William Shakespeare, Twelfth Night

"So hallowed and gracious the time," Shakespeare wrote about the night of Jesus's birth. In the Christian Year, time itself becomes holy and full of grace. *All* time. That is the importance of the Christian Year: it makes all time holy.

Growing up in the Southern Baptist branch of the Free Church stream of Christianity, I became aware that the Christian calendar fought for time with the civic calendar. The three major holy days in most Baptists churches were Christmas, Easter, and Mother's Day. The lesser, but not much lesser, feast days were New Year's Day, Father's Day, July Fourth, Labor Day, and Halloween. I speak whimsically, but the point, I hope, is made.

On New Year's Eve we had a "Watch Night service" that ended at midnight. The Watch Night service began to wane when Baptists started talking to each other in liquor stores and New Year's Eve parties took precedence over the worship service.

Mother's Day Sunday was a high celebration of motherhood, often honoring the youngest and oldest mothers in the church. As I've learned through the years, Mother's Day can be a very painful day for many reasons, so if Mother's Day is recognized during worship, it should be done to celebrate the manifold ways those in the congregation nurture children, youth, and adults inside the church and in the community.

The July Fourth service was an annual event for many churches. Baptist professor of preaching Clyde Fant tells of when he recently went with his mother to a July Fourth service at his home church in Texas. Three flags flew on the tall flagpole: the American Flag, the Christian Flag, and the Texas Flag. Which was highest? He said, "Jesus and Texas tied for second." His quip brings up the serious business of the relationship of Church and Nation in worship. The move to bring the American flag into sanctuaries is a recent phenomenon, beginning for most churches in America around the time of the Second World War.

Halloween usually was celebrated by a fall festival party at church, with no mention of All Hallows' Eve, All Saints' Day, or All Souls' Day. Growing up Southern Baptist, our only saint was Lottie Moon, the heroic missionary to China in whose honor we took the Lottie Moon Christmas Offering for Foreign Missions every December.

Needless to say, the Christian calendar was of far less significance than the civic calendar. The concept of sacred time was minimized, except for the priority of Sunday as the day of worship. Only in later years has the Baptist Free Church discovered the spiritual treasures of the Christian Year. First came, in some churches, the celebration of Advent, later came the observance of Lent, and later still Pentecost Sunday.

In the history of Christian worship, first came the establishment of Sunday as the day for worship. By the mid-second century, as we have seen in Justin Martyr's description of early worship, Sunday became the Lord's Day because God on the first day began creation, and, more significantly, on the first day Christ rose from the dead. From the institution of Sunday as the day of worship came the development of the Christian week. Every Sunday was the celebration of Christ's resurrection, and every Friday was a day of fasting in remembrance of Christ's death. From the Christian week came the development of the Christian Year.

The earliest annual festival observance in the second century was the Easter Feast, preceded by the Triduum (Three Great Days) in remembrance of the Paschal Mystery of the death and resurrection of Jesus in the three separate but continuous services: the Maundy Thursday Service with the Eucharist, the Good Friday Service of Darkness on the day of Jesus's crucifixion, and the Easter Vigil on Easter Eve. Later came the celebration of the Nativity with Christmas Eve and Christmas.

Today, for many of the Baptist Free Church, the sacred year of the Christian calendar has become primary, beginning the first Sunday of Advent. The season of Advent prepares for the coming of God in Christ. The longing for God is at its heart; "As a deer longs for flowing streams, so my soul longs you, O God" (Ps 42:1). The universal longing for God to come in peace and heal the world is expressed in liturgy and song as we prepare for Christ's coming into the world.

The Season of Epiphany follows in the new year. It is a season to remember the ways Jesus "manifested" (the meaning of the word "epiphany") the glory of God in his ministry. I call it the season of light, water, and miracles.

The Season of Lent focuses on our baptismal identity, on the meaning of the Christian life, and can be used as a time of preparation for baptism and the renewal of baptismal vows, which I have discussed in my book *Baptism: A Living Sacrament of the Christian Life*.[1]

Today, more churches in the Free Church Tradition observe a Holy Week encompassing more than the two days of Palm Sunday and Easter by including one or more of the Triduum. I have led Maundy Thursday Communion services remembering the Last Supper that have been simple and meaningful. Many of my churches have observed Good Friday in profound and moving ways. In my present church, we have sponsored a Good Friday Peace Walk, walking together to some of the places where people have been deeply damaged by the racism and injustice in our city. For us, the Peace Walk is a way to unite Jesus's crucifixion with all the suffering and crucified people of the world. The Passion of Christ and the Passion of the world become one.

Gail Ramshaw calls the Easter Vigil "the Queen and mother of all Christian liturgy."[2] Early in my ministry I adapted an Easter Vigil service that has been tailored for use in some of my churches. It begins with the Great Fire of Easter on the front porch of the church. From that fire the congregation's candles are lit, and we all process into the darkened sanctuary while someone sings the Exultet, the ancient song of praise that announces the manifold gifts of Easter.[3] Then there is a set of readings from the Old Testament recalling God's mighty acts of creation and deliverance. Next comes the reading of Jesus's baptism, a service of baptism, and the renewal of baptismal vows or the baptismal covenant. Finally, we experience the climax of the service as the Easter Gospel is read and the first Easter hymn is sung.[4]

Eastertide is composed of the seven Sundays of Easter and emphasizes the power of the Risen Christ in the life of the church and our personal lives. Wendell Berry ends one of his poems with the words, "Practice resurrection."[5] In Eastertide, we practice resurrection during worship with the reading of texts of Jesus's resurrection appearances and passages in the book of Acts, which tell of the church alive in the power of the Spirit in the presence of the Living Christ.

Pentecost celebrates the coming of the Holy Spirit upon the church in Jerusalem, and Pentecost Sunday offers us the opportunity to reflect on the presence and meaning of the Holy Spirit. The next Sunday is Trinity Sunday, and we ponder the meaning of God who is Three in One. We celebrate God as a community, and we are invited to join in the perichoresis, the divine circular dance of the Father, Son, and Holy Spirit. To speak poetically, God is so One and Threeful, so Threesome and One.

On the first Sunday in October, many churches celebrate World Communion Sunday. This day encourages worldwide Christian unity and seeks to embody Jesus's prayer that "we may be one." It is a good day to speak of the Ecumenical Movement, which began in Scotland more than a century ago and works to overcome the scandal of a badly divided church.

The last dates I mention in the Christian calendar are November 1, All Saints' Day, which honors the saints and martyrs of the church through the centuries, and November 2, All Souls' Day, when we remember those who have died in the local community. In most Protestant churches, the Sunday closest to these days is celebrated as All Saints' Sunday, which honors those in the congregation who have died. It is also the Sunday when we celebrate the Communion of Saints who have guided us through the years.

It is important for the church to honor the meaning of sacred time. There are two Greek words for time. The first is *chronos*, tick-tock time, clock time, chronological time. The other is *kairos*, which stands for times of great significance, revelatory and salvific time. Kairos is the way the Bible speaks most about time. The "Day of the Lord" was the day of salvation and deliverance. Mark captured Jesus's preaching as he began his ministry: "Jesus came to Galilee proclaiming the good news of God and saying, 'The time is fulfilled, and the kingdom of God has come near'" (Mark 1:14-15). Kairos time. In his hometown sermon, Jesus proclaimed the acceptable year of the Lord, the year of God's favor, and said that time of deliverance was "today," now! In 2 Corinthians 6:2-3, Paul quotes Isaiah 49: "At an acceptable time I have listened to you, and on a day of salvation I have helped you." Then he exclaims, "Look, now is the acceptable time; look, now is the day of salvation!"

The Greek word for "Now" is "Nun" (pronounced "noon"), and it sounds like the tolling of bells, "Nun, Nun, Nun!" Like the bells on church steeples announcing worship on the Lord's Day, like the Angelus in some churches that begins worship with the ringing of the bell three times in celebration of the Father, Son, and Holy Spirit, like bells on Christmas Day filling the streets, like bells in a monastery calling for the praying of the hours, like the bells on Easter morning, saying, "He is risen!"

Ring them all, and enter into the sacred time of the Lord! It is the time of grace. It is salvation's joyful now.

Notes

1. H. Stephen Shoemaker, *Baptism: A Living Sacrament of the Christian Life* (Macon, GA: Smyth & Helwys, 2022).

2. Gail Ramshaw, *Reviving Sacred Speech* (Akron, OH: OSL Publications, 2001), 86.

3. One exemplary contemporary rendering of "Exultet" is found in *The United Methodist Book of Worship* (Nashville: The United Methodist Publishing House, 1992), 371–72.

4. An order of worship for my Easter Vigil service is in my book. Shoemaker, *Baptism*, 107–109.

5. Wendell Berry, "Manifesto: The Mad Farmer Liberation Front," in *The Selected Poems of Wendell Berry* (Washington, DC: Counterpoint, 1998), 87–88.

Chapter 21

On the Planning of Worship and Other Practical Matters

Praise ye the Lord; 'tis good to raise
our hearts and voices in his praise:
his nature and his works invite
to make this duty our delight. —Isaac Watts[1]

Over the course of my fifty years of ministry, I have had the extraordinary experience of planning worship with gifted and dedicated church musicians, clergy colleagues, worship committees, and worship boards. We have learned together, and I have received many blessings from them. I could not have written this book without them.

In many of my churches, the ministers and the church musicians on staff have met together on Monday of each week to read and share our insights into the texts of the next Sunday. I offered them the direction of the sermon. Through these conversations, we planned worship together. We discussed anthems, hymns, and the liturgy of the service. We pooled our wisdom, and the week was set!

These weekly meetings were possible in churches with a staff present at the church. But even when those leading worship were not able to meet weekly, we found a way to meet regularly. This long-term planning was also possible because early in my ministry, I developed a habit of outlining my sermon themes and texts for three months or more in advance and then giving that schedule to everyone involved. I've found that as the habit developed, sermons from the lectionary texts, sermons that addressed particular topics, and often whole sermon series would spring to mind, building my enthusiasm for the year ahead. The needs of the hour might from time to time necessitate a change in my preaching schedule, but overall, this advance planning on my part made planning seasonal and weekly worship better for everyone.

When planning a series of sermons, I have been energized by the way church musicians reinforce my preaching with musical selections that lead worshipers in a sort of cumulative effect. A series of sermons on the Lord's Prayer, for example, featured a different musical setting of the Lord's Prayer sung by the choir or congregation each week. It deepened my worship as well as the congregation's.

After many such planning meetings, I created a planning sheet that covered all the essentials to discuss for each Sunday's worship. A sample page is included in Appendix III.

On the Three-Year Common Lectionary

The Revised Common Lectionary has been a great gift to churches across denominational lines. The resources available to aid in the use of the lectionary are rich and plentiful, such as the *Handbook for the Revised Common Lectionary*,[2] which includes each Sunday's texts for the day—the Psalm, the Old Testament reading, the Epistle and Gospel readings—and offers anthem and hymn recommendations. I have also found the *Handbook*'s index to be helpful for Sundays when we have chosen a text outside of the lectionary order. To be sure, the lectionary's music selections reflect the worship traditions of mainstream Protestant churches in America, so pastors and church musicians in other traditions must adapt the music suggestions to their own congregation's needs.

There are alternative lectionaries available now that seek to fill in the gaps of the Revised Common Lectionary. One is the work of Wilda C. Gafney, a Womanist biblical scholar, in her *A Women's Lectionary for the Whole Church* (2021), which has its own three-year format.

There are contentious issues in churches today, just as there have always been contentious issues. Some of today's are music selections, projection screens, inclusive language, and applause in worship. I remember a cartoon of an usher handing a bulletin to a person coming into worship and asking, "Would you like the Clapping or No Clapping Section?"

It is all too easy for those in the "No Clapping Section" to become like David's wife Michal, who scolded David over his exuberant, ecstatic dancing before the ark of the Lord (see 2 Sam 6). The "No Clappers" can make worship become like a classical music concert where educated insiders know we are not supposed to applaud between movements of a piece of music and look down their noses or stare reproachfully at the "unlearned" who clap between the movements.

How do we negotiate these potential minefields as ministers, musicians, and congregations? The Apostle Paul's words to the Corinthian church's conflict over issues like glossolalia (speaking in tongues) in worship can guide us today, 2,000 years later (see 1 Cor 10–13). Here is how I would apply Paul's teaching.

Whether the issue is applause, song choice, or inclusive language, our guiding principle must be that which Paul gave to the church at Corinth: "'All things are permitted,' but not all things are beneficial" (1 Cor 10:23). That is, we are free to do anything—anything that builds up the Body of Christ. At Corinth, the main issue at hand was speaking in tongues, which, while appropriate and helpful in private devotion, was not always so in public worship. Paul instructed them that the interpretation of tongues should accompany ecstatic speaking in tongues. Then the whole body is built up. How might we apply that counsel today to the issues in our own churches?

Let's take the issue of applause in worship as an example. In the Pentecostal church, worship, often ecstatic as the Holy Spirit moves among the people, includes speaking in tongues, shouts of joy, dancing, lifting of hands, and sometimes applause. "Clap your hands, all you peoples," the psalmist declared (Ps 47:1), and applause can be an act of joyous praise of God. Such ecstatic worship is not generally contentious among Pentecostals because the whole congregation sees it as edifying.

But to the other churches in America, applause is not edifying. It distracts and interrupts the worshipers. Some see it as irreverent, or they may see it as exalting a performer instead of God. One worshiper may feel their applause is appropriate for their experience in worship; they need an exuberant response to God. Others may hunger for a moment of quiet contemplation at those moments, and their worship is hindered.

There is no biblical rule against applause, but unless it is edifying to the whole, it is counterproductive to worship. What, then, does love require of us when issues such as these become contentious? How do we bow to the needs of the other? Paul wrote to the Galatians,

> For you were called to freedom, brothers and sisters, only do not use your freedom as an opportunity for self-indulgence, but through love become enslaved to [servants of] one another. For the whole law is summed up in a single commandment, "You shall love your neighbor as yourself." (Gal 5:13-14)

We are free to do what is loving for God and for each other. Each church then must pursue not applause or silence, not screens or hymnbooks, but love. Or, to paraphrase Paul's magnificent words to the church in Corinth:

> If I sing with the ecstatic tongues of an angel or preach in the full measures of my mind's powers but have not love, I have become fingernails scratching down a chalkboard.
> If I applaud 'til my palms sting or sit on my hands and have not love, I am not worshiping.
> If I insist on inclusive language, or if I insist on the language of King James, and have not love, my words are only noise.
> If I think my way of worship is the only true way to worship, I have not love, and I have become merely a worship critic.
> If I enjoy classical music or prefer praise songs and I have not love, I am worshiping my preferences rather than God.
> Love is patient and kind toward my brothers and sisters in church. It is not envious or boastful or rude. It does not insist on its own way; it is not irritable or resentful. Love endures all things, hopes

all things, and bears with one another in all things. Love always wins the day. (see 1 Cor 13)

So, my friends and fellow disciples in Christ, take time to talk with one another, minsters, musicians, and congregation. Learn together what worship means and how it best serves all the people. Come to holy agreement—and leave room for those who disagree. As Paul urged, make "every effort to maintain the unity of the Spirit in the bond of peace" (Eph 4:3). Then let us praise the Lord with one accord!

One day our best human worship, and all its words and songs, will pass away, and all that is left will be love, and we will be lost in wonder, love, and praise. May the love of God, the grace of our Lord Jesus Christ, and the beloved community of the Holy Spirit be with you all.

Notes

1. Isaac Watts, "The Divine Nature, Providence, and Grace," https://hymnary.org/text/praise_ye_the_lord_tis_good_to_raise.

2. Peter C. Bower, eds. *Handbook for The Revised Common Lectionary* (Louisville, Kentucky: Westminster John Knox Press, 1996.

Living Water and Broken Cisterns— Toward the Renewal of the Church in the Renewal of Worship

I am finishing this book on January 25, the Feast Day of the Conversion of St. Paul, who amid blinding light and astonishing grace was called by Jesus to be his apostle. He never got over the grace of God, and nor will I, no matter how many words I write.

People are worried, if not alarmed, about the state of the church in America. Churches are hemorrhaging members, offerings have plummeted, and church ministry staffs are shrinking. Since the pandemic, many have chosen to spend their Sunday mornings elsewhere. Yet I am reminded of Mark Twain's cable from London back to the American press after his obituary was published in error: "The report of my death was an exaggeration."

As we have seen in the history of Christian worship, reformation and renewal of the church has happened over and over again. We have seen the Protestant principle at work as expressed in its slogan: "the church reformed and always being reformed." Moreover, these periods of renewal and reformation have been at least as much about renewal in worship as in theology. Such may well be true today: the church will find renewal in the renewal of worship. It begins in every congregation, small and large.

I started in this book with the conversation between Jesus and the Samaritan woman. She had gone to the well to draw water. Jesus appeared to her and offered her "living water," water that would become in her "a spring of water gushing up to eternal life." She replied, "Sir, give me this water, so that I may never be thirsty" (John 4:14-15). This is our cry. We come to worship seeking this spring of water, the living water welling up to eternal life. Jesus is the source, and we seek to be a worthy vessel receiving and offering it to others. It is never a perfect vessel, and we trust with Paul that we carry such a treasure in our crackable clay pots to show "that this extraordinary power belongs to God and does not come from us" (2 Cor 4:7). In true worship everything points to God and to Christ. With all we are, we seek to worship in spirit and in truth.

Sometimes in the history of God's people, we get our worship wrong. Why would we not from time to time? Jeremiah the prophet said to God's worshiping people these words from God:

> For my people have done a two-fold wrong:
> They have forsaken Me, the Fount of living waters,
> And hewed them out cisterns, broken cisterns,
> Which cannot even hold water. (Jer 2:13, Jewish Study Bible)

But God has been faithful to be present in worship at all times and places and in worship of many wonderful and diverse kinds.

This is a time of beauty and peril for the church. It is a time of crisis as depicted in the Chinese pictogram, a combination of the words "danger" and "opportunity." Ours is a time of dangerous opportunity. It is a time to discern what to throw out and what to keep. Phyllis Tickle has said that every 500 years the church has a huge rummage sale. We are about five hundred years from the Protestant Reformation, so we might be right on time. This is a propitious time, even a time of Kairos, to discern what to keep and what to throw out; to ask, "Can we repair that cistern, or do we need to build a new one?" Or to ask with Jesus, "What are the old wineskins to put aside so we can have new wineskins that can hold the new wine of what the Spirit is giving us today?" (see Matt 9:17).

This is a time of challenging spiritual discernment. Where is living water, and where are our cisterns so broken that they cannot hold it? Jesus told the woman at the well, " Woman believe me, the hour is coming when you will worship the Father neither on this mountain nor in Jerusalem" (John 4:21). Those words challenge us and point us where we might go and how we might worship today. In this book I have hoped to give guidelines for such discernment. There are enduring principles of Christian worship that can still guide us, but the true paths forward will be revealed by God and the Spirit, paths that are given to each congregation in its setting. We will need qualities of mind and spirit that you may have glimpsed in this book, even as through an imperfect pane of glass:

Kindness	Reverence
Honesty	Respect
Humility	Freedom
Boldness	Wonder
Creativity	Love
Inclusion	Praise

I have offered guidance to understanding the meaning of each element of worship, but these are not captured by any set form of worship or the province of any one worship tradition. They are like the notes on a scale with which we make our own music, the standard chords for which the improvisation of jazz arises.

When worship renewal comes, it will come as pastors, ministers of music, lay leaders, and the whole congregation enter into holy conversation about worship. Take worship and hymn surveys. Talk about what is most important to the congregation in worship or about moments in worship that have moved them. Be brave. Put it all on the table. Seek God's help.

For leaders of worship, the renewal of worship, as the planning of every Sunday's worship, will require hard work and bring deep pleasure. Annie Dillard describes what it feels like when after so much hard work, a word, phrase comes, coming as all God's gifts, as "unmerited grace":

It is handed to you, but only if you look for it. You search, you break your heart, your back, your brain, and then—and only then—it is handed to you. From the corner of your eye, you see motion. Something is moving through the air and headed your way. It is a parcel bound in ribbons and bows; it has two white wings. It flies directly at you; you can read your name on it. If it were a baseball, you would hit it out of the park. It is that one pitch in a thousand you see in slow motion; its wings beat slowly as a hawk's.[1]

We are in search of the best worship we can offer as we seek God, yet we may discover that God is already in search of us. As the old hymn sings,

I sought the Lord, and afterward I knew
He moved my soul to seek Him, seeking me.
It was not I that found, O Savior true.
No, I was found of thee. (Jean Ingelow, 1878)

Worship is searching for God and being found. It is our duty and delight. It is living water, the pitcher, and the lamp. May God bless the work of your heart, soul, and mind, your hands and your imagination, and may you this day "be filled with the Spirit, as you sing psalms and hymns and spiritual songs to one another, singing and making melody to the Lord in your hearts, giving thanks to God the Father at all times and for everything in the name of our Lord Jesus Christ" (Eph 5:18-20).

Soli Deo Gloria

Note

1. Annie Dillard, *The Writing Life* (New York: Harper and Row, Publishers, 1989), 75.

Appendices

Appendix I: Modern Worship Anthems

Modern worship has given us the gift of anthems and songs of worship that voice all parts of a soul brought before God. Here are some examples:

<u>Anthems of Praise</u>
"My Eternal King," Jane Marshall
"All People That on Earth Do Dwell," Vaughan Williams
"The Majesty and the Glory," Tom Fettke
"Come Thou Fount of Every Blessing," Mack Wilberg, arranger and composer
"O Clap Your Hands," Vaughan Williams—and many other anthem settings of this Psalm text

<u>Anthems of Thanksgiving</u>
"Litany of Thanksgiving," John Ness Beck
"i thank You God for most this amazing day," Dan Forrest, a setting of the e e cummings poem

<u>Anthem of Supplication</u>
"I Need Thee Every Hour," John Ness Beck

<u>Anthem of Lament</u>
"Out of the Depths," Martijn de Groot

<u>Anthem of Praise and Resolve</u>
"God of Grace and God of Glory," Paul Langston

Anthem of Prophetic Utterance
"God Bring Thy Sword," Ron Nelson, Samuel H. Miller

Anthem of Christian Experience
"Ev'ry Time I Feel the Spirit," William Dawson, arranger

Anthem of Discipleship
"He Comes to Us," Jane Marshall, setting of the last paragraph of
Albert Schweitzer's *The Quest of the Historical Jesus*

Appendix II: Order of Worship from Scottish Free North Church

This is a sample order of worship from the Festival of Psalms at Free
North Church, Inverness, Scotland, on Saturday, September 7, 2024.

Order of Service
Welcome
Ps 122: (Scot Ps) St Paul
Opening Prayer
Introduction of the Psalms
Ps 63:1-5 (Scot Ps) Bays of Harris
Ps 1(b):1-6 (Sing Ps) St Petersburg
Introduction of the Psalms
Ps 117:1-2 (Sing Ps) Regent Square
Ps 85:1-13 (Sing Ps) Dim Oud Jesu
Introduction of the Psalms
Ps 124(2nd):1-8 (Scott Ps) Old 124th
Ps 134(b):1-3 (Sing Ps) Servants (*seated*)
Prayer
Introduction of the Psalms
Ps 23 (Stuart Townend) Accompanied
Ps 130 ("I will wait for you") (*seated*)
Introduction of the Psalms
Ps 143(2nd):6-8 (Scot Ps) Heber
Ps 107:23-31 (Scot Ps) Lochbroom

Introduction of the Psalm
Ps 107:29-30 (Gaelic) Kilmarnock (*seated*)
Introduction of the Psalms
Ps 16:7-11 (Sing Ps) Golden Hill
Ps 29:1-4, 10-11 (Sing Ps) St. Denio
Introduction of the Psalm
Ps 34:7-11 (Sing Ps) Land of Rest (*seated*)
Thanks to the presenters and contributors
Ps 24:7-10 (Scot Ps) St George's, Edinburgh (with "Hallelujah, Amen")
Prayer and Benediction.

Appendix III: An Aid to Planning Worship

Calendar Date	Liturgical Date
Text	Special Emphases
Topic	Hymns
	1 2 3
Worship Leaders	Worship Music
Announcements: Call to Gathering: Invocation: Prayers of the People: Scripture: Other:	Prelude: Solo: Anthem: Offertory: Postlude:
Notes:	

Appendix IV: New Hymns for Today's Church

Ruth Duck, "Wash, O God, Your Sons and Daughters" (a Baptism hymn)

Brian Wren, "I Come with Joy to Meet My Lord" (a Communion hymn)

Brian Wren, "Bring Many Names"

Fred Pratt Green, "When in Our Music God Is Glorified"

Fred Pratt Green, "For the Fruits of this Creation"

Jeffrey Rowthorn, "Lord, You Give the Great Commission"

Jaroslav Vajda, "God of the Sparrow, God of the Whale"

Shirley Erena Murray, "Lift High the Cross"

Shirley Erena Murray, "O God, We Bear the Imprint of Your Face"

John Bell and Graham Maule, "Will You Come and Follow Me if I but Call Your Name"

Jane Parker Huber, "For Ages Women Hoped and Prayed"

Jane Parker Huber, "Christ Has Called Us to New Visions"

Jane Parker Huber, "On Pentecost They Waited"

Fred Kahn, "For the Healing of the Nations"

Graham Kendrick, "Shine Jesus Shine"

Appendix V: Exemplary Hymnbooks and Song-books for Worship Planning and Private Devotion

The Worshipping Church (Hope Publishing Company, 1990).

African American Heritage Hymnal (GIA Publications, 2001).

Church Hymnary (Canterbury Press, 2005). This remarkable Scottish hymnal begins with a long selection of Psalms set to music and contains global church songs, American hymnody, including gospel songs, and hymns and songs from the Iona Community as well as Scottish hymns.

The Chalice Hymnal (Chalice Press, 1998).

The United Methodist Hymnal (United Methodist Publishing House, 1989).

Celebrating Grace (Celebrating Grace, 2010).

The Faith We Sing (Abingdon Press, 2000; Hymn Supplement).

A New Hymnal for Colleges and Schools (Yale University, 1992). This hymnal offers an especially beautiful setting of George Herbert's "King of Glory, King of Peace" (#434).
Rejoice in the Lord, ed. Eric Routley (Wm. B. Eerdmans Publishing Company, 1985).
Common Ground: A Song Book for All the Churches (Edinburgh: Saint Andrew Press, 1998).
Ritual Song: A Hymnal and Service Book for Roman Catholics (GIA Publications, 1996).
With One Voice: A Lutheran Resource for Worship (Augsburg Press, 1995; Hymn Supplement).
Glory to God (Presbyterian Publishing Company, 2013).
A Covenant Hymnal: A Worshipbook (Covenant Publications, 1996; Evangelical Covenant Church).

Appendix VI: Template for a Service of Worship on the Meaning of Worship

The following uses resources from this book and worship music examples.

Silent Meditation
Print the words of St. Symeon The New Theologian and the Description of Second Century Worship by Justin Martyr.
Prelude
Opening Sentences
From Isaiah 6:1-3:
Leader: In the year that King Uzziah died,
I saw the LORD high and lifted up sitting on a throne;
and the hem of God's robe filled the temple.

People: Above God stood the seraphim;
and one called to another and said,
"Holy, holy, holy, is the LORD of hosts;
the whole earth is filled with God's glory"

Hymn of Praise
"Holy, Holy, Holy"

Invocation
The Spoken Word
> *short 5-minute meditation*
> "The Doxological Self: Praising, Blessing, Thanking, Awe, and Delight"

Song
The Prayers of Confession
The Spoken Word
> "The Self in Lamentation and Confession"

Song
> "I Need Thee Every Hour" (solo, hymn, or anthem)

The Reading of God's Word
> Colossians 3:16-17
> Matthew 4:1-4

Anthem
The Spoken Word
> "The Dialogical Self: The Self and Church in Conversation with God"

An Affirmation of Faith
Spoken Word
"The Beseeching Self: The Self in Intercession"
The Prayers of the People
Spoken Word
> "The Eucharistic Self: The Self that Receives, Gives Thanks, and Shares the Grace of God"

The Offering
Offertory Anthem
> "Come Thou Fount of Every Blessing"

The Doxology
The Service of the Table
> Prayer of Thanksgiving
> Prayer for the Spirit
> Commemoration and Words of Institution
> Sharing of the Bread and Cup
> Prayer after Communion

Spoken Word
  "The Apostolic Self: The Self Called, Sent, and Blessed"
The Hymn of Dedication
  "Guide Me, O Thou Great Jehovah"
The Charge, Benediction, and Blessing
Postlude

www.ingramcontent.com/pod-product-compliance
Lightning Source LLC
Chambersburg PA
CBHW062213080426
42734CB00010B/1866